Real Food Pantry Makeover

NOURISHING YOUR FAMILY

A Word of Wisdom Perspective

on

Health, Happiness, & Success

THE
HEALING PLACE

www.JenniferDayley.com

To Heavenly Father – For answering my desperate plea & leading me down the unexpected path of holistic living. For lifting me up & making me strong enough to be who I was meant to be, and for giving us all the beautiful wonders of nature that provide healing, happiness, & peace.

To Kirk – For marrying me, having faith in me when I didn't think I could go on, & encouraging me to reach for the stars. For sacrificing your own comfort to work endless hours to support us, & for bragging to your friends & co-workers about my food. You are my rock.

To Jessica, Chylanne, Ashlynn, & James – For quite possibly teaching me more about life than I've taught you. For telling me you love me in front of other people, & continuing to call me 'Mommy,' even though you're not little anymore. For being patient in my healing process, & for constantly bringing your friends over to taste-test my recipes.

To My Mentors – (You know who you are)… For teaching me that abundance means so much more than just money. I'm so grateful that because of you, I am able to now see why I have never been drawn to competition. Thank you for helping me begin to stand in my power, so I can help others stand in theirs.

Contents

The Recipes

Chapter 1

Introduction

"Houston...we have a problem."

Depression, anxiety, diabetes, fibromyalgia, cancer, ADHD, chronic fatigue, obesity, lupus, immune disorders, IBS, allergies, heart disease, high blood pressure, Obsessive Compulsive Disorder, tooth decay, hearing loss, appendicitis, tonsillitis, candida. People feel stressed, broke, under-educated, overworked, entitled, hopeless, lonely, lazy, unorganized, lost, tired, sick . . . .

Blagh!!!

The list goes on, and on, and on . . . . What has happened to us? Do you know someone who fits somewhere in there? Do YOU fit somewhere in there? Things are a little out of control, and I think it's high time we do something about it. As it stands right now, we need all the help we can get. If you're reading this book right now, there is a reason. Don't stop. Keep going. If you're struggling with health, emotions, or chaos, I'd like to tell you something: **You really will be okay.**

I CAN'T DO THIS ANYMORE!

As I stood at the edge of the Snake River Canyon, with uncontrollable tears streaming down my face, gazing at the river below me, I contemplated and wondered if it was worth even being here anymore. I humbly and hopelessly looked up at the sky and said, "I can't do this anymore. I'm done. I really am. If you want me to do what you sent me here on this earth to do, you're going to have to take over. Give me different answers. Tell me where to go from here, because I give up." (And then, after about an hour, I wiped my face, walked back to the car, and drove home to my family.)

That's what I said to God in the summer of 2009 because I was sick and tired of being miserable. For the purposes of this particular book, I won't go into all of the details of my life and what I went through; but there are a few things I'd like to touch on with you. I was ready to be done with the "dis-eases" I'd been dealing with for so long. In addition to the emotional health issues – including depression, anxiety, and Obsessive Compulsive Disorder – I was nearly 50 pounds overweight, when I'd been thin all my life. I had surgery and was in the hospital nine times for bowel obstructions in just a couple of years' time.

I'd had enough of 18 years of pharmaceutical pills and their "side" effects. (I actually don't believe in "side" effects. To me, they're just effects.) I was back and forth between therapists. Nothing was working. Doctors performed all the typical tests, and everything came back negative. Ugh! My last doctor had no answers except to keep trying different medications and send me to more counseling.

Little did I know the "anything but mainstream" road my Heavenly Father would put me on shortly thereafter. The funny thing about it all is that, He started me down the road before I ever even said that prayer, but I didn't know it. That's often how it works, though. Things are being created and laid out in front of us, even when we're not aware of it and don't see what's going on.

It took some time for this simple concept to become clear in my mind and heart; but I finally realized that, even when we think all is lost and there's no hope left, the Lord is working behind the scenes on our behalf, to pave the way for our success and abundance.

He's putting the pieces of the puzzle in front of us, so we can gather them along the way and complete the picture—with His help. He's providing us with the pen and paper, so that we can write our story—with His help.

Though God knows the big picture and all of His purposes will be fulfilled, He allows us to create the story of our lives. If our will is in line with His will, then we are able, with Him, to co-create a magnificently beautiful story.

My personal belief is this: If our desires are righteous, if our motives our pure, if our hopes and dreams are unselfish and reached for in humility, then what we want for ourselves and our families will be what He wants for us. He's right there, ready to receive our requests and ready to give abundantly, if we are just willing to ask, have faith, be patient, and take action when inspiration comes.

We make it more complicated than it really is, honestly. We do! We allow C.H.A.O.S. (Can't Have Anyone Over Syndrome) to creep in and take over. God is simple and operates on the concept of "order in all things." Wouldn't it be lovely if we could all have simplicity and order in our lives? I think we can, even when chaos is going on all around us. We can have order in our own bodies and in our own homes.

In this book series – and my more in-depth, online Let's Get R.E.A.L. Course – I'm going to show you how to say good-bye to chaos. I'm going to help you learn how to take your life back, get organized, and own your own power. You'll learn how to keep your body as non-toxic as possible, how to nourish yourself, how to be organized, how to be prepared in a healthy way, and how to live a fulfilling life. You may think it's super duper hard, but that's really only your perception and false beliefs getting in the way. Don't worry. I do it myself sometimes, too. We're human, right?

The great thing is, I don't do it nearly as much as I used to because I've learned how to see life differently, taught others to do the same, and am now sharing how with you. The concepts are simple. It's just a matter of learning what they are and how to utilize them in a step-by-step manner. You have the power to do this. You have the power to better yourself; and through that process, you have the power to change generations!

This book series is for any of you who suffer from any kind of negative "anything." It's time to get rid of that junk and allow abundance of all kinds into your lives. Whether it's health, relationships, finances, personal development, or spirituality, the principles I'm going to teach you can be used individually and collectively in all of these areas. When a principle works in one area and can be applied in other areas as well, you'll know it's a true principle. If you have faith and take action by applying that principle, you will succeed. Along with these principles, you'll receive no-nonsense tools and baby-step systems for making "getting there" much easier.

I've been where you are. I know what it's like. I've jumped the hurdles. I've made the mistakes. I've been stuck and gotten unstuck. I've failed and succeeded. And I'm here to help you, because my mission in life (next to being a wife and mom) is to serve others through teaching what I know. In serving others, I'm also serving God, which is my number one priority. I'm an actively Christian, homeschooling mom who's passionate about all things creative, healthy, holistic, organized, and spiritual.

We tend to do important, life-changing things for two reasons: desperation and inspiration. In my case, it was both. I was desperate to overcome the health challenges I had and wanted to be happier. I felt I had no other choice but to do the opposite of what I'd been doing all my life. If you're doing the same exact thing over and over, expecting different results, you're going to be very disappointed. Once I started making changes, inspiration came flooding in, and I couldn't help but want to make even more changes. It was exciting and much easier than I thought it would be. If you are desperate now, the time to change is now. But if you're not desperate yet, then why wait until you BECOME desperate? Why not START NOW and prevent future misery? Taking one step at a time is easy; and, in this case, it can even be fun!

My husband and several friends and family members have pushed me to write a book for a long time now. I have always loved writing, but it's not something I thought I'd ever actually do professionally. However, in working with my clients and talking with people in my everyday life, I realized there is a huge need out there! So many are lost and don't even know where to start in improving their lives. I'm constantly getting asked how to get started in eating real food, how to organize the kitchen, and how to heal common ailments, naturally. I knew it was time to get out the pen and paper (or computer and keyboard) and create books and an online course, to share my experiences and knowledge and save others the time and hard knocks I had to learn on my own. People need help! Here is that help.

After several years of both personal experience and research, I've learned that our physical, mental, and emotional "dots" can easily become disconnected and cause great chaos. As a Life Designer, I teach holistic and faith based principles and strategies to help people re-connect the dis-connect and Calm the Chaos in their bodies, minds, and homes. Wouldn't you love to experience more health, peace, order, and abundance in your own life? Abundance is so much more than monetary. I know that now, and it's very humbling. And exciting. And peaceful. Health, relationships, finances, recreation, education, spirituality, personal mission, and much more are all a part of living abundantly. There are many people in this world (think 3rd world countries) who have very little money but live much more abundantly than some millionaires! They know what's really important in life, and they're HAPPY.

God was and still is a part of my journey. I teach these principles from a spiritually based Christian perspective. God created us, the earth, and the food we eat. He is the reason we heal and are successful in the things we accomplish. It's because of Him that I've been able to make changes in my life and end up where I am today. He continues to carry me through this ongoing journey, so I can end up where He wants me to ultimately be. If you simply take it a step at a time with His help (or jump in 100% and change everything today, if that's what you want to do), you will experience miracles. I promise! Let go of the fear of failing, and remember that the ONLY way we fail is if we don't try. If we're really trying, then failing is only a stepping-stone to the next success.

Don't be that person who misses out on life's opportunities, good health, and happiness. Don't be the person who denies your family the knowledge to do the same. Be the person others marvel at! Stand in your power and be the one that causes others to say, "How does she/he do that?" Take action, improve your life, and inspire others to do the same!

Chapter 2

Out of Order

So what is causing all of these negatives in our lives? Some experts say it is stress, and I don't completely disagree with them. However, I learned something important a few years ago when I was taking a whole food health course that I'd like to share with you.

ONE DIS-EASE

Not hundreds. Not thousands. Just <u>ONE</u>.

· **Chaos - Atomic level**

causes

· **Chaos - Molecular level**

causes

· **Chaos - Cellular level**

There is ONE DIS-EASE. Not hundreds. Not thousands. Just ONE. CHAOS. Chaos means "out of order," hence the word "dis-order." And most of the time, stress is caused by chaos. So really, chaos is what it all boils down to. I like this acronym to describe CHAOS: **C**an't **H**ave **A**nyone **O**ver **S**yndrome. Can you relate? CHAOS seems to be a normal part of life these days, but often times it catches us off guard and throws us for a loop. Let me show you what I mean.

When our cells are in chaos, our bodies & minds are in chaos. I don't know about you, but when I'm not feeling in control of myself or my health, I feel anxious and stressed, which causes me to want to "check out" of life and forget everything. I definitely feel like I "**C**an't **H**ave **A**nyone **O**ver"! I don't have the energy to entertain, I don't want others to see the state I am in, and I feel vulnerable, embarrassed even. That is the power of chaos, and it is influenced largely by the health of our cells. What we put in our bodies, on our bodies, and around our bodies affects every single cell God gave us. We're either feeding our cells in a positive way that's for our highest good, or we're hindering our cells from doing their job and functioning properly. Think for a minute about what that means to be either nourishing or hindering our cells. We have skin cells, brain cells, hair cells, blood cells; in fact, our entire bodies are made up of cells. So when you are hindering those cells – hindering your brain, your blood, your organs, etc. – it manifests in every area of your life, in the form of the many "dis-eases" you see all around you. One of the most important ways to keep our bodies and minds in a peaceful and balanced state is by eating the right foods. Healthy food creates healthy cells, which create healthy brains, healthy blood, healthy organs, etc. Do you see the connection between our food, our cells, and our health—mental, emotional, physical, and spiritual? Pretty powerful, isn't it?

Through my business, The Healing Place, I've been able to help many people just like you climb out of life's slumps, move forward, and thrive despite the chaos around them. The tools I've used over the years to get my own life in order are some of the tools that I'm now able to share with you, so you can finally do the same. You don't have to live a life of chaos. Your body can be at peace, your mind can be at peace, and your home can be at peace.

Life is holistic. Holistic means universal, comprehensive, and whole. Holistic living embraces timeless principles and tools that God provided to help us thrive right from the beginning. I'm going to show you how to use those principles to create order (the opposite of chaos) in your own life. I could tell you that I'm going to share the "secrets" to getting healthy and living abundantly in this book, but there really are NOT any secrets here. These are just simple tools that have worked time and time again throughout history, and you are fully capable and deserving of embracing them yourself. How would it feel to be balanced in body, mind, and spirit? How would it feel to actually feel good? How would it feel to have hope? I would like to help you with that.

There are really only

3 causes of the ONE dis-ease (Chaos):

1. **Toxicity**
   - poisons your body
2. **Deficiency**
   - of vital nutrients
3. **Imbalance**
   - of emotions & energy
     Caused by trauma/thoughts & beliefs

So if you address these causes, you automatically address the dis-ease. That's it. It's that's simple. I think sometimes we make it more complicated than it needs to be. My goal is to help you shift into "simplicity thinking," letting go of making things so complicated, or at least thinking they are. **The fuel you give your body is either working for you or against you.** It was working against me and my family for many years, and it took desperation to get me to change. If you're not to the desperate point yet, don't allow yourself to get there. Make changes NOW.

> *"The food you eat can either be the safest and most powerful form of medicine or the slowest form of poison." – Ann Wigmore*

There's a "don't tell me what to eat and how to live my life" stigma out there, and everyone's sort of gotten set in their modern/western/industrialized ways. Culture is funny sometimes. We get stubborn. Clear and simple methods of holistic living that have been proven to work over the centuries somehow got crowded out by modern life. Though there have been wonderful advancements in technology and emergency/modern medicine, can we say that we're really much better off than we were 100 years ago in terms of health and stamina?

(Hint: The answer is no.)

In a lot of ways, we're worse. We've gotten so hung up on the laziness of just accepting what media and masses tell us. We've put our blinders on, and we're not learning for ourselves and taking responsible action to improve our personal wellbeing. We'd rather, as a whole, take the easy way out. What we don't seem to understand is that taking the easy way out usually results in things being harder in the long run. Or maybe we **do** understand it, but we're still choosing the immediate results over the lasting results. (We've basically become impatient and lazy!) I know that's hard to admit. I can say that, though, because I <u>was</u> that person.

I've learned that in order to live life to the fullest, I've got to embrace new (old) ways of thinking. Though it seems to be a slow process, society is finally waking up and realizing that holistic and healthy living are not ridiculous, hocus pocus, or woo-woo pseudoscience for the uneducated. Honestly, it's been exciting (I say that humbly, of course) to have simple opportunities to dumbfound a few western medical professionals the last couple of years . . .

"Yes, I really did heal my cavities without going to a dentist."

"Yes, we do get rid of strep throat and bladder infections without antibiotics."

"Yes, I did heal my chronic bowel obstructions myself, ditched the meds, and never returned for another colonoscopy they insisted I'd be doomed to for the rest of my life."

"Yes, I have helped clients get rid of gall bladder problems, years of knee pain, and emotional issues without the use of pharmaceutical medications or surgeries."

It's nothing to be offended by or afraid of! Eastern and Western cultures need to meet in the middle and work together. That's all there is to it. We really can be friends!

Now, as we look at how to overcome "chaos" and "dis-ease" in our lives, notice that the first two causes of chaos are food-related: getting rid of toxins and getting sufficient amounts of the right nutrients. So it seems only appropriate, in terms of the causes and how our health affects everything else in our lives, to start with FOOD.

Make no mistake – this is more than just a recipe book. I'm going to teach you how to heal your relationship with food. I'm also going to show you how to easily bring delicious, real homemade food into your home, so you can gather your family together and soak in the nostalgia of togetherness, enjoy the explosion of all your senses, and inspire those around you by the changes you've made. That's in addition to getting healthier, feeling better, and "changing the world"—one step and one person at a time. Remember: That one person starts with you!

If you've never done anything like this, believe in yourself. You CAN do it! Wherever you are in your dietary choices and holistic lifestyle, there are principles and tools here that will bless you and prepare you for more abundance in every area of your life. So let's get started!

Chapter 3

To Please the Eye and Gladden the Heart

Remember when? I sure do! I was born and (mostly) raised in the South. My roots are in Georgia. My favorite home in the whole entire space system was my Grandma and Grandpa Kelly's little red brick home with pecan (pronounced "pee-can") trees in both the front and back yards. Early in the morning, we would visit them and be greeted with the mouthwatering smell of fresh, hot breakfast. Eggs, toast, bacon, orange juice, and coffee were the norm. I don't drink coffee; but to this day, that is one of my favorite smells. It brings back memories of pure, unadulterated LOVE.

My Grandpa Fred often walked across the church parking lot behind their house, over to the store in the mornings; and he would take my sister and me (still in our pajamas) with him to buy us bubble gum. I still remember the smell of the pine trees and the sound of the woodpeckers. After we returned back to the house, he would help us fix our breakfast. Now granted, they did eat some processed & artificial foods, including cereal. He had preparing that cereal down to an exact science. First the bowl. Then the milk. Then the Sweet 'n Low. Then stir. Then the cereal. In that order. But for the most part, I remember good old-fashioned, fresh, homemade Southern food. And we ALWAYS sat at the table together, blessed the food together, and ate together.

Southern Farmer's Markets were heaven. They were usually the little "side of the road" produce stands that accepted cash and check (or trade). My grandparents bought fresh peaches, corn on the cob, boiled peanuts, okra, and other garden goodies. I remember one day when my grandpa let me sit in his lap and drive his truck to the cornfields. We came home with loads of sweet baby white corn. That was the best corn I've ever tasted. And it wasn't genetically modified.

Peaches. Oh, those Georgia peaches… Close your eyes for just a minute. Imagine yourself bringing a fresh, juicy, just-picked peach up to your mouth and sinking your teeth into it. Taste it. Smell it. If not a peach, then your favorite fruit or berry. Live in the moment! I don't know about you, but just the mere thought of eating a fresh peach floods emotions and memories into my mind. To me, it's heaven in my hands.

Conscious eating (or purposeful eating) is what I like to call this momentous food experience. When you're taking the time to pay attention to your food, its smell, its taste, its texture, and feeling gratitude, you're eating with purpose. You'll find yourself eating slower, chewing better (which is healthier anyway), & actually enjoying it more than what most people do anymore. Instead of gorging yourself with large bites & eating faster than what your brain & belly can register, you'll become fuller faster, & you'll be satisfied more quickly. This is helpful for better nourishment & weight loss, and even being more in touch with your emotions.

I remember one day when my mom spent all day in the kitchen making homemade, whole wheat bread. These days we don't "have" to spend all day in the kitchen making bread, with powerful mixers like Bosch at our disposal. In fact, it takes me about two hours to make three extra-large loaves. But she spent several hours in there that day, and we had what seemed like 10 or 11 loaves. It was probably only three or four; but to me, it felt like we were highly abundant in bread! I remember that smell, too. Fresh butter spread across the top. Mmmmmm . . . . I don't know if she knows this or not, but it was so irresistible that particular day that I ended up eating ½ a loaf all by myself. Her food was *almost* as good as my grandma's food. (It's okay. I've already had that conversation with her, and she's at peace with it.)

After a handful of personal food disasters of my own, I was able to eventually catch the vision and succeed with real food also. In fact, my very first experience with cooking food on my own after getting married did not turn out well. At all. I placed two chicken thighs (gag) in a Tupperware container, filled it halfway with water, sprinkled the top with white table salt, and pushed our microwave's "START" button. Yes, that was our dinner. Not one of my fondest memories, but let me tell you something: If I can graduate from boiled, microwaved chicken thighs to writing a book on real food, ANYONE can learn how to cook and eat properly. No excuses.

My grandpa and grandma were perfect examples of bringing the family together for physical, emotional, and spiritual nourishment. I'll be forever grateful that they passed that knowledge and tradition onto my own mom, so that I could live in at least some kind of real food environment, remember it, and finally embrace it for both myself and my family. The memories and emotions of real food at home are fresh at the forefront of my mind, my nose, and my heart.

"Your body is the instrument of your mind. In your emotions, the spirit and the body come closest to being one. What you learn spiritually depends, to a degree, on how you treat your body." – Boyd K. Packer

How do you feel about food? When you think about eating, do you stress because you're not sure what to cook or eat? Do you worry about whether or not it's good for you? Do you eat because you're bored? Do you eat because you're stressed or worried? Do you use food as a comfort to make up for something you feel you're missing in your life? Are you afraid to make changes because it is overwhelming to you, or because you don't think you have enough money to eat healthy?

Much of life revolves around food. It's the very thing that keeps your body functioning. Without food, you would lose your life. Without the correct foods, you will likely lose your life sooner than what you otherwise would if you were nourishing yourself the right way. Since we feel emotions of some sort nearly 100% of the time, it's only logical that food and emotions would intertwine at some point, right?

Culturally, food is used to celebrate. Sometimes it's used as a reward for successes or given as gifts. It brings people together. When we see or smell a beautiful dish or farm-fresh produce, it lifts our spirits and brings us joy. It puts a smile on our faces.

"Yea, all things which come of the earth, in the season thereof, are made for the benefit and the use of man, both to please the eye and to gladden the heart; Yea, for food and for raiment, for taste and for smell, to strengthen the body and to enliven the soul."
– *Doctrine & Covenants 59:18-19*

On the other side of the coin are the more negative associations we have with food. Over-eating is tied to the emotions of anger, resentment, tension, emotional protection, craving closeness, and desire to show power. Under-eating is tied to the emotions of feeling like you can't live up to other people's expectations, self-rejection, lack of spiritual understanding and knowing who you really are, and subconsciously desiring to self-destruct due to lack of love for yourself.

Many people use food (or other things such as money) as a substitute to cover up the pain they're experiencing. If you desire to change the way you eat and begin making transformations in your family's kitchen, yet you feel that it's too hard for you to do because your emotions are tied to the food you eat, then pray! If you have an addiction to a certain food or drink, ask God to help you work through and ultimately overcome the addiction.

If you have an eating dis-order, ask God to help you find help in overcoming the dis-order. If you're eating to replace emotions you don't want to deal with, ask God to help you overcome the inability to deal with your emotions. Do not turn to food for help, especially unhealthy, processed, adulterated foods. These foods actually CAUSE unnatural appetites because of the addicting chemicals that are contained in them. Food is POWERFUL. So keep them out of your system and turn instead to a stronger Power to help bring you and your body to healing and joy in your food.

Besides suggesting you pray, I would ask you this question: How committed are you to getting yourself on a healthy path? Do you remember me talking about "why" I wanted to make changes? Don't forget about your "why." Write down the reasons. Get emotional about it. The "why" is the one thing that will help you overcome your natural man/negative physical tendencies surrounding food. Remember – at first, my "why" came out of desperation; then my "why" was because of inspiration. Consider the answers to these questions as you write your "why."

"I want to be healthy because...."
"I want to honor and nourish my body because...."
"I want to teach my children how to honor their bodies because...."

Are you afraid that you'll have to give up good-tasting foods to eat healthy? I promise, you don't. Healthy foods taste better. Most people who eat real food that's been cooked and prepared the right way think it tastes better immediately! You have more options with real food. Once you start eating real food, you'll literally FEEL the difference in a very short amount of time, and you won't want to go back to your old ways. Any addictions you may have (sugar, chocolate, bread, salt, etc.) will go away, and you will begin craving fruits, vegetables, whole grains, and other real foods. The wonderful thing is, it will satisfy you! That is something that fake food CANNOT do. Ever.

My husband and I were talking recently after "having" to eat at a restaurant, about how the food we just ate literally had a low vibration to it. It was almost as if we could feel the atoms in the food moving slowly instead of vibrantly. The energy of the food was sluggish and left us feeling completely unsatisfied and yucky. We even tried to choose healthier options with lots of vegetables, but it didn't make a difference. It contained additives, was cooked at high temperatures, and was anything but fresh. We knew in a very short time that our bodies were not reacting well to what we were putting in them.

Our bodies are constantly talking. Lie detectors measure subtle energy in the body by monitoring & recording muscle response. Through Applied Kinesiology, brought to the US in the 1960's by George Goodheart, we are able to read those energy responses without the use of a machine. Blocked energy flow gives a weak response, where freely flowing energy gives a strong response. It can be done with any muscle, but is most commonly and easily done using an arm or fingers. If I were to muscle test yourself, you would put a piece of food in your hand and stretch your arm out to your side. I would put light pressure on the top of your wrist as you resist my pushing down on your arm. If your muscle response to whatever we're testing is strong, your arm will stay up, and you will be able to resist my pressure. That means that your body is recognizing positive energy in the food in your hand, something it wants and needs. If your response is weak, however, then you will not be able to hold your arm up, no matter how hard you try. It will fall to your side as I push your arm down. That is your body telling you that the food in your hand is not what it needs.

When I teach classes and speak at conferences, I often do a muscle testing demonstration to show my students how their bodies react to different foods. I first test them holding fresh well water in a glass bottle, and then I test them holding a plastic bottle of soda pop. Without fail, their muscles go weak when holding the soda pop and stay strong when holding the water. The same thing happens when I test them with a fresh, organic apple vs. a candy bar. Your body knows, energetically first, what is beneficial and what is not. Then when the food goes into your mouth and begins digestion, your body will either recognize the food and know what to do with it, or it will not. Even a strong football player will get weak when handed a low-energy food that his body does not want or need.

Why does this work? Everything in existence is energy, including food. In 1992, Bruce Tainio developed the method for measuring the body's frequency. This equipment also measures the frequency of food. He determined that when the body's frequency dropped, the immune system was compromised. If you're putting low-vibration or low-energy food into your body, it is going to lower your body's vibration or energy. This will adversely affect your immune system and your health.

Take a look below at the difference in frequency levels between live foods and dead foods. Please note that fresh food and herb levels can be higher if grown organically and eaten freshly picked:

Fresh Foods and Herbs 20-27 Hz
Dried Foods and Herbs 15-22 Hz
Processed Foods 0 HZ (Majority of industrialized nation's food supply)

Low-energy food, with nearly non-existent frequency, doesn't do anything positive for your body. In fact, it does the exact opposite. Your body doesn't even recognize processed & adulterated food. There are actually organized patterns in real food that can be seen under a microscope. But there are no patterns in processed food, and it looks like complete chaos. Nature is full of patterns and symbolism, and it is balanced and organized.

William Coles (1626-1662 AD) was a 17th Century botanist, herbalist and physician. He authored a book titled *The Art Of Simpling*, which explained that the appearance of plants provided clues (or signatures) to certain parts of the body that indicated its beneficial medicinal use. Modern-day researchers are now (<u>Finally</u>!) focusing more on the study of whole foods as healing foods. Eaten in the right quantity, whole foods can literally reverse and prevent disease. This "Doctrine of Signatures," originally dating back to the writings of Galen (131-200 AD), is just fascinating. Take a look!

- **Carrots (sliced):** Look like the human eye. The pupil, iris, and radiating lines look just like the human eye. And YES, science shows carrots greatly enhance blood flow to and function of the eyes. Carrots contain beta-carotene (hence their orange color), which reduces the risk of developing cataracts.
- **Celery, Bok Choy, Rhubarb, etc.:** Look just like bones. These foods specifically target bone strength. Bones are 23% sodium, and these foods are 23% sodium.
- **Mushrooms (sliced in half):** Look like a human ear. Adding them to your diet in sufficient quantity actually improves hearing function and quality.
- **Ginger:** Stomach = Nausea = Enough Said! A study from the *European Journal of Gastroenterology and Hepatology* shows that ginger stimulates digestion by speeding up the movement of food from the stomach into the upper small intestine.
- **Kidney Beans:** Look like, heal, and help maintain KIDNEY function. They look just like a kidney. They're a rich source of fiber, folate, and magnesium. They help lower bad cholesterol and reduce the risk of kidney disease.
- **Heads of Lettuce, Broccoli, Cauliflower, and other Leafy Greens:** Look like and assist in head/brain health! They even prevent cancer.

The Journal of Neuroscience suggests the chemical sulforaphane, which is found in broccoli and other cruciferous vegetables, can help boost the condition of the blood-brain barrier if it is damaged.

- **Coconut:** Is hard just like a skull. It has "hair" just like a head. It has three indentations (holes) and looks just like a little face. Inside the coconut is the memBRANE (brain). It is now known that coconut is one of the most beneficial foods for brain health and function. Coconut oil is imperative for those with diseases such as Alzheimer's, Parkinson's, ALS (Lou Gehrig's), Multiple Sclerosis, and Diabetes. A must-read for Alzheimer's treatment is a book written by Dr. Mary T. Newport, M.D., called, *Alzheimer's Disease: What If There Was a Cure?*
- **Onions:** Look like the body's cells. Onions clear waste materials from all of the body's cells. They even produce tears that wash the epithelial layers of the eyes. Coincidence?
- **Tomatoes:** Usually have four chambers and look just like the human heart. Tomatoes contain lycopene (which means RED) and are, indeed, pure heart and blood food. Lycopene reduces the risk of heart disease and cancer. Lycopene has been found in studies to help counter the effects of unhealthy LDL cholesterol.
- **Avocados:** Look just like and target the health and function of the womb and cervix of the female. They balance hormones, help shed unwanted birth weight, and prevent cervical cancers. It even takes exactly nine (9) months to grow an avocado from blossom to ripened fruit!
- **Olives:** Look like ovaries and target the female reproductive system. They assist in the overall health and function of ovaries.
- **Figs:** Are FULL of seeds and "hang in twos" when they grow. They increase the mobility of male sperm and increase the number of sperm to overcome male sterility.
- **Walnuts:** Look like a little tiny brain with two hemispheres. They contain significant amounts of omega-3 fatty acids. Walnut extract can break down protein-based plaques associated with Alzheimer's. Walnuts are also said to enhance signaling within the brain and encourage new messaging links between brain cells.

- **Grape Clusters:** Grow in the shape of lungs. Lungs are made up of branches of airways with tiny bunches of tissue called alveoli. They resemble bunches of grapes. They allow oxygen to pass from the lungs to the blood stream. Grape seeds also contain a chemical called proanthocyanidin, which appears to reduce the severity of asthma triggered by allergies.
- **Sweet Potatoes:** Look like the pancreas and actually balance the glycemic index of diabetics and help the pancreas to support the body's ability to process and break down sugars the correct way.
- **Citrus Fruits:** Inhibit the development of cancer in human breast cells. Cut them in half and notice the specific similarities in the shape and details inside AND out.
- **Bananas:** Look like a smile! They contain a protein called tryptophan, which, once digested, is converted into the chemical neurotransmitter, serotonin. Serotonin is a mood-regulating chemical in the brain. Most anti-depressant drugs work by adjusting levels of serotonin. Bananas are also beneficial for symptoms of PMS!

"There is not a cellular unit, organ, or body system that does not have its counterpart in that which we call plants."
– Original Source unknown

Oh the kindness of our God to be so mindful of us through His creations.

Chapter 4

Anything but Mainstream

Food storage, ya'll. Prepping. That's where it started. I've been fascinated with the concept of being self-reliant since not long after I was married in 1992. Our basement and pantry were stacked with several canning jars and #10 cans of food, in case of emergency. I wouldn't consider myself a die-hard "prepper," but I was genuinely interested in taking care of my family in hard times, come what may. In 2008, I began researching preparedness. In the process, I came across some information about "healthy" food storage. Huh??? Wait . . . there was an actual training course on this stuff? Oh yes, there sure was. And it spoke to me. I knew there was something I needed to learn from it, so I dove in.

The next few years were baby steps. At first I switched our family to whole grains and added more beans into our diet. I got a little bit addicted to learning, and I think my subconscious brain knew the information I was downloading would lead me to more answers for healing. Over time, researching healthy food storage led me to learning about real food, non-toxic living, natural healing, the laws of abundance and purposeful living. Such simple, timeless principles; and yet they seemed so foreign to me! Little did I know I would eventually end up teaching classes in my home, to local groups, and at out-of-state conferences about these same things I was learning. I realized in all of my learning and teaching that all of these things are a part of preparedness. Prevention of physical, emotional, and spiritual chaos is what preparedness is all about.

Come 2012, I was excited about what I was learning but quite frustrated, because I was still on medications, and I was still overweight, no matter what I did to change it. It was extremely discouraging. I just wanted to feel better, look better, and get off those pills.

Amid my research, I came across a holistic living conference, and my eyes became fixated on a class taught by Carolyn Cooper, founder of the Simply-HealedTM Method of energy work. Some people call it energy medicine, energy therapy, or energy healing; but it's all essentially the same thing. In short, it is a combination of removing emotional blocks, rewiring the subconscious brain to let go of limiting beliefs while integrating new positive beliefs, & balancing the energy systems in the body to create homeostasis.

As unfamiliar as energy work was to me at the time, I was completely drawn to it & thought about it constantly. Little did I know, I'd become a certified practitioner myself & then train others in my own IDEALife INNERgy Method just a few years later. You can find out more about this method of healing at www.jenniferdayley.com.

Many hospitals now offer energy work before and after surgeries and other procedures because of its ability to calm people's bodies and minds and assist in quicker healing.

I had tried ditching the medications two or three other times, and I never could do it, even with the doctors trying to wean me off. But shortly after my session with Carolyn, I decided to cut my medication in half; and it was easy! My Naturopathic Physician (a doctor who specializes in healing the whole person vs. only treating symptoms and diseases) assisted me in coming off the rest of the medications in only <u>FIVE</u> months, which is amazing, because normally it's a 1-2 year process. Personal experience here. She supported my body with herbs and nutrients in addition to more emotional release (energy work), which kept me in balance. Over that same time period, through learning about natural living and real food, we went from 11 medications between four of my family members to only ONE medication for ONE family member. It was incredible!

At that point I knew I had to make some more changes for this to be lasting. It had been nearly four years since I started my journey into this new world, and I'd taken a lot of baby steps up to this point. Something was telling me I needed to take a bigger step (no—a big LEAP) into the world of holistic living and real food.

The one (and first) book that changed my perspective about food was, *The Word of Wisdom–A Modern Interpretation*, written by a well-respected scientist named John A. Widtsoe. Granted, things have changed a little in the past 70+

years since it was first written; but overall, the things I learned about eating real food and using non-toxic products are timeless, and nearly all of what that book contains is still truth! This book taught me about the SPIRITUAL importance of food and treating our bodies the way God designed. Yes, the physical aspects of eating healthy are important, but there is so. much. more.

Let's go back in time for a minute and answer these 10 questions through the scriptures:

Q: Adam and Eve first lived in where?
Answer: A Garden

Q: What was the first test given to the first people that God placed on the earth?
Answer: Partaking of the fruit

Q: What are some of the very specific laws talked about in the beginning books of the Old Testament?
Answer: Dietary laws

Q: When Christ introduced the Sacrament, what was the object He used?
Answer: Food and drink

Q: What was the setting when He introduced the Sacrament?
Answer: The Last Supper

Q: What was one of the most significant miracles performed in the bible?
Answer: Feeding fish and bread to the 5,000

Q: What was used in healing throughout the scriptures?
Answer: Herbs

Q: What was the term used to describe followers of Christ who bring other people to Him?
Answer: Fishers of Men

Q: How did Daniel prove to the King that he would "gain knowledge and skill in all learning and wisdom"?
Answer: By refusing the King's meat and wine, and instead eating the food the Lord instructed him to eat

Q: What is a significance of the word Gethsemane?
Answer: Gethsemane means "Olive Press"

That's just a small sampling of the many profound instances where food is used in the scriptures. I think maybe food is important! In fact, take a look at this list of a few religions that implement food-based health codes in their teachings and practices:

The Church of Jesus Christ of Latter-day Saints
Seventh-Day Adventists
Buddhism
Hinduism
Judaism
Islam

What I've found through studying various practices of health is that there are many (and I mean MANY) differing opinions on what kind of food is good for us. Think about it. How many times have you gone to a bookstore or the library and actually found books or articles that completely agree with each other on what is healthy to eat? **(Ahem. I see very few of you raising your hand.)** It's no wonder everyone is confused!

- "Dairy is bad for you."
- "Fruit is bad for you."
- "Green smoothies are bad for you."
- "Soy is bad for you."
- "Potatoes are bad for you."
- "Nuts are bad for you."
- "Eggs are bad for you."

- "Oil and fat are bad for you."
- "Meat is bad for you."
- "Wheat is bad for you."
- "Heck, all grains are bad for you!"

I personally can't keep up with all that mess. Everyone thinks they're right. Yet are we getting healthier as a people? Are we improving overall? NO. Most of us are suffering from (or know someone who is suffering from) some kind of degenerative or emotional/mental dis-ease or dis-order. It's time to use our brains. Logic, please!

Germ dis-eases aren't the big problem anymore, my friends. Chronic and degenerative dis-ease, which are mostly preventable by proper nutrition and staying non-toxic, are the big problem these days. Modern sanitation, clean water, and hygiene have greatly reduced the germ problem. And if your environment (your surroundings and your body) is properly nourished and free of toxins, then it's much easier to fight off the big bad attack of the germ and often prevent it altogether. Those who are healthy are most often able to overcome illnesses without lasting consequences. After all, let us not forget the words of Louis Pasteur at the end of his life: *"Bernard was right; the pathogen is nothing; the terrain is everything."*

Chapter 5

Dear Family, There's Something I Need to Tell You

So what are we to do with all this confusion? How do we know what to eat? For a very sick person with debilitating dis-ease, it may not be as simple, at least at first. I personally don't believe in "diets" **except** in the case of healing. Sometimes extreme measures need to be taken in order to bring the body back into a state of homeostasis (balance). However, I do believe that healing diets should not be permanent. These temporary diets may include eating raw foods, going dairy/gluten free, etc. It all depends upon the individual and their particular circumstance. Those situations should be taken up with a health care professional who specializes in nutritional therapy and healing diets.

What I'm emphasizing here, though, is what we should be eating in general to prevent dis-ease, overcome most illness and dis-ease, gain more energy, get rid of depressive states, be calmer, and YES be more spiritual. Don't let the world of food-fuss confuse you! Don't obsess over whether you're eating perfectly or not. The <u>stress</u> is going to do you more harm than simply eating as well as you can.

From a Christian perspective, the Lord's Atonement is Infinite. When we are truly doing our very best, and if we are grateful for and bless the food God has provided for us, we can be assured that God will cover our lack and make up the difference. Yes, even with food.

My Faith's health code, the Word of Wisdom, emphasizes a mostly plant-based, whole food diet—eating meat sparingly, and abstaining from all harmful and addictive substances. As I read John Widtsoe's book and really started delving into studying it, I realized I wasn't even close to living it. I also realized it wasn't just about me getting skinnier or getting off medications. There was much more. Our physical state affects our mental/emotional state, so obviously both of those would affect our spiritual state, too. And since they all work together, all three need to be balanced in order to thrive and be able to do what we're meant to do in this life.

The spiritual growth I've had since really implementing God's system of nourishment has been more than profound. It's REAL. When it finally hit me, I was on fire! Nothing mattered to me more than doing what I knew God wanted me to do. He wanted me to honor and respect the temple He gave me, so that I could fulfill the mission He sent me here to fulfill. **He wanted me to live on purpose!** And he wanted me to teach my family and those around me about it, too. He wanted me to live up to my potential and, as my faith's health code promises, to "run and not be weary" and "walk and not faint."

> *"Know ye not that your body is the temple of the Holy Ghost which is in you, which ye have of God, and ye are not your own? For ye are bought with a price: therefore glorify God in your body, and in your spirit, which are God's." – 1 Cor. 6:19-20*

I was so done with baby steps and measly little changes. I just wanted to get this thing done! So I rolled up my own sleeves, and off to the kitchen I went. After about 30 minutes, my counter was piled with food, and my pantry was completely empty. Trash bags were filled up with "questionables" that weren't even worth keeping, yard sale boxes got stacked full of stuff to sell, and a few things went in my "food storage" stash (for emergencies; or, if nothing else, for trading).

That day, I took the plunge. And...I had to tell my family. Let me tell ya. It's interesting to watch the looks on your kids' and husband's faces when you tell them you threw out all the white sugar. And when you tell them they won't be eating boxed cereal in the morning anymore. And when you tell them that they would never find another bag of Doritos, Oreos, Cheerios, or

Quaker Granola Bars in the pantry again. And when you tell them that you'd be making them milkshakes and smoothies with **green** vegetables. I regret that I didn't videotape those moments.

No really, they were actually pretty good about it. They knew the few things I'd changed over the last few years tasted good, and they were willing to give it a shot (with just a little hesitancy and heartbreak). But the transition went pretty smoothly I think, compared to what it could have been.

My kids do still choose junk food once in a while when they're not at home. What's beautiful about the whole thing, though, is that they're making **informed** choices. They know ahead of time that junk food is not going to sit well with them. Instead of being forced to only eat nourishing foods, they can choose for themselves and reap the consequences, whether they're negative or positive. The important thing is that I've taught them. I've done my best to lay the positive foundation in our home for good health instead of bad health, so my children can make good choices and hopefully avoid the pitfalls of bad health & shortened lives later on.

> *"The fathers and mothers have laid the foundation for many of these diseases, from generation to generation, until the people are reduced to their present condition.... The people have laid the foundation of short life through their diet, their rest, their labor, and their doing this, that, and the other in a wrong manner, with improper motives, and at improper times. I would be glad to tell mothers how to lay the foundation of health in their children, that they may be delivered...." – Journal of Discourses 2:269-71*

My life is forever changed, but what's even better is that as my children continue to be as healthy as possible, the effects they're going to have on their children and future generations are profound. As the light bulbs went on, I realized that **this wasn't just about me.** This was about my **posterity** and anyone else who was ready to listen to and learn what I've been blessed to learn and teach. The potential of the ripple effect could be infinite! The ripple effect: It's REAL.

Chapter 6

The Showdown – Low Down

There is junk, and there is food. Commercial food products are not natural. They're fake, and they're toxic. If it was created in a lab, processed in a factory, or raised in confinement, it's not as nature created it, your body will not recognize it, and it will have negative effects on you, one way or another. Period.

I'm not even going to begin to try and prove the negative effects of these fake foods, because you will find contradicting answers wherever you look, including so-called "studies." I am using the common sense God gave me and sharing my own knowledge and personal experience over the last few years. If you're interested in more "proof," I highly recommend *The Food Babe Way*, by Vani Hari. It's one of the best books I've read on what's really hiding in your food. Of all the modern books I've read on nutrition, her book is actually closest to my beliefs about food. There's nothing really extreme diet-wise about her, just good ol' common sense. I love Vani!

One more thing I want to emphasize is that you're on a journey. You're learning how to make changes in your life. Change means to become. Every person is going to "become" in a different way and at a different pace. I hereby give you permission to use the "good-better-best" formula. Let me give you an example of this:

Bad – Store bought white or wheat bread.
Good – Homemade white bread using dry commercial yeast.
Better – Homemade whole-wheat bread using dry commercial yeast.
Best – Homemade soaked/sprouted whole-wheat bread using **natural** yeast.

Note: I don't really think white bread is good for you, even homemade, but it's the easiest example I could come up with for this illustration. Do the best you can. If you know your choice isn't very good, be strong and try stepping it up a notch. Stay there for a while until you're used to it, and then try stepping it up again. Some people call it "raising the bar." I encourage you to stretch yourself as much as you can, but don't—I repeat, DON'T—beat yourself up (or give up) if you feel stagnant or even move in a backward direction at times. There's always room for improvement, and **the only way you can fail is if you quit or don't try.** Remember that.

Now, as I suggest these changes from junk to real food, let's talk "diets" for a minute. I don't believe in them, and I think they cause confusion and even negative health problems. Vegetarianism is great in my opinion, because you're limiting meat or not eating it at all, but you're still receiving the benefits of live animal foods. I'm fine with that! We've cut a good 90% of our meat consumption out of our family's diet. We still eat some cheese, yogurt, kefir, sour cream, and real butter. We've reduced our milk intake from 1 gallon per day to 1 gallon per week AT MOST. We consider it a food, not a drink, and the milk we do drink is now farm fresh and raw. Water is our drink of choice. Water should be everyone's drink of choice! We do our best to keep animal food consumption to 10% or less of our family's diet.

I'm not a "100% Vegan" fan, either; it requires people to use supplements to get their B-12 and K-2. God didn't design us to **have** to use supplements. He gave us everything we need to be completely nourished in the form of real food and herbs. I personally feel that – unless you're on a specific, temporary healing diet – entire food groups, if they're real food, should not be cut out of one's diet. Except in the case of meat; I'm okay with cutting out meat. But don't worry if we're not on the same page, I won't judge you. Everyone's in a different place, and that's perfectly fine.

Do you count calories? Do you count sugar intake, salt intake, fat intake, and all that other mumbo-jumbo on the back of food labels? Did you know that **YOU DON'T HAVE TO**? Think about it. No one in history used to read and calculate food labels. Why should we? If you're eating real food, your body is going to naturally recognize it and know what to do with it. And if you're not eating an excessive amount (or have emotional issues you need to release), you're going to maintain a healthy weight.

I think it's ridiculous that we're eating unhealthy, fattening packaged food products and worrying about calories when we could be just eating real food and not even thinking twice about calories! Doesn't the thought of not having to pay attention to any of that sound nice? **The only thing you should have to pay attention to on the back of food labels are the ingredients and the number of servings.** Most of the packaged food and drinks you consume are actually 2-3 servings instead of one. But they don't inform you of that on the front of the label, so most people eat or drink the whole thing because they don't check the back! That means you're getting 2-3 times the servings you should, and yet the food is still not satisfying. Remember, you may be full, but **"you can never get enough of what you don't need, because what you don't need can never satisfy you."**

Speaking of labels, do you even KNOW what's in your food? I hate to break the news, but if you're eating what's on approximately 80% of grocery store shelves, you're eating pesticides, hormones, antibiotics, chemicals, preservatives, artificial sweeteners, artificial colors, artificial flavors, addicting sugars, dead processed grains, endocrine disruptors, synthetic vitamins, rancid unhealthy fats and trans fats, MSG, neurotoxins, heavy metals, genetically modified organisms, carcinogens, and more. There are over 10,000 ingredients <u>added</u> to our food! The FDA has never reviewed over 3,000 food chemicals; and as far as food labels go, more than 5,000 substances aren't even required to be labeled!

- **If your great-grandparents would not recognize it as food - it's probably not real food.**
- **If it was created (or raised) in a factory or confinement - it's probably not real food.**
- **If you can't pronounce and don't recognize the long list of ingredients on the label - it's probably not real food.**
- **If you can't grow it, gather it, milk it, or hunt it - it's probably not real food.**

If a food product has vitamins in the ingredients list, you are getting synthetic vitamins that have been added back into the food. This is what "enriched" means; and it's done because, as the "food" has been adulterated, the natural vitamins that were present in any of the original real food components have been completely destroyed. Why would they do that? It doesn't even make sense. Who wants synthetic? Synthetic is fake! What happened to real? Our cells do not recognize synthetic.

Other than the hundreds of chemical constituents and parts that God naturally combined in perfect proportions to make up "original" foods (Gosh, He was smart!), real food contains **ONE ingredient:** the food itself.

Apple = Apple
Milk = Milk
Peanut = Peanut
Coconut = Coconut
Brown Rice = Brown Rice
Honey = Honey (and pollen, if it's raw and unprocessed)

Yes, we can take several whole foods and combine them to make other foods, like breads, salads, sauces, casseroles, etc., BUT there are still just those few simple ingredients. Not boat loads of processed foods and toxic chemical concoctions our bodies don't recognize or know what to do with.

Often times companies will state one or two things on the package that are true (to make the food look wholesome); but they do it to deliberately take your attention away from the fact that there are many other toxic ingredients in the list, in attempt to make you believe that it's healthy, hoping you won't notice. **Addicting ingredients are deliberately added to food to keep you coming back for more.** Again, fake food may fill you up, but it will never satisfy you. And they know it. Dishonesty and greed are running rampant in our current food system.

"If these substances are abolished by man, how can the large numbers of people who will be thrown out of employment be cared

for? The most obvious answer is that moral evil is NEVER justified by economic good. It may also be answered that the money now expended for these injurious substances would more than care for the unemployed in a state of idleness." – John A. Widtsoe, Scientist

Maybe let that sink in for a few minutes.

Now, what I'm about to show you is, in my mind, unreal (no pun intended). For those who eat and store pre-made/packaged/processed food products, I would like to show you just a few examples of how many ingredients you are getting. **Please note that most of the ingredients in these food products are artificial, genetically modified, and toxic.** One other fact most people don't realize is that MSG (a highly-used neuro/excitotoxin in foods) is usually disguised and hidden by one of about 40 other names. There are those who will argue that MSG is in breast milk and other natural foods, so it must not be dangerous. What they don't realize is that there are different forms of MSG. What's in breast milk is not the dangerous, chemically-formed kind, as explained in the article about MSG & glutamic acid on the Eden Foods website.

Here we go. I walked through the grocery store and counted ingredients myself on the labels of several popular foods. I also looked up restaurant food labels on the Internet and researched books and articles. I made a long list, and I was sickened. I knew our food was bad; but until I started actually looking at labels when I started down this "change my life" road a few years ago, I had no clue it was this bad. It blows my mind that this is what my family used to "nourish" our bodies with. Take a look at just a FEW of the things I found:

- Chick-Fil-A chicken sandwich (better than a burger, right?) - OVER **100** ingredients
- Subway 9-grain bread (healthy, yes?) - **50** ingredients
- Yoplait "light" strawberry yogurt - **14** ingredients
- Sun Chips - **30** ingredients
- Hidden Valley Fat Free, Cholesterol Free and Gluten Free Ranch Dressing - **30** ingredients

- Homestyle seasoned herb croutons - **45** ingredients
- Kashi Go Lean Crisp - Over **30** ingredients
- Top Ramen Noodles - Over **30** ingredients
- Pizza Hut Pizza (depending on which pizza) - up to **100+** ingredients
- Marie Calendars Homestyle Creations (stuffing and turkey) - **70** ingredients
- Kroger "Hearty" Vegetable Broth - **14** ingredients
- Van Kamps Pork and Beans - Over **15** ingredients
- Morning Star Vege Burgers - **35** ingredients
- Campbell's Healthy Request Savory Vege Soup - Over **35** ingredients
- Lean Cuisine - Average **50** ingredients
- Lunchables - Average **50** ingredients
- Pringles - Sour Cream and Onion - up to **34** ingredients
- Eggo Nutrigrain Whole Grain Low Fat Waffles - Over **25** ingredients
- Smart Balance Margarine - **19** ingredients
- Birds Eye Voila 3 Cheese Chicken - **50** ingredients
- Green Giant Broccoli and Rice Steamers - **30** ingredients
- Quaker Granola Bars - **43** ingredients (including 9 different sugars)
- Hot Pockets - Over **50** ingredients
- Whole Grain Lean Pockets - Over **100** ingredients

Now we're going to take on the big guns: Elimination. Let's begin with the most difficult one of all, the one everybody seems to be addicted to these days. I know, I know—Grab yourself some tissues, wrap up in a blanket, and tell yourself you can do this. Remember what I said earlier? "Everything is going to be okay."

Here's a quick run-down of what I would encourage you to work toward eliminating from your kitchen completely. If you're one of those who can make the clean sweep all at once, great! It's fairly obvious, though, that most people aren't there yet. If you have to, choose one thing and at least start somewhere. Just a note, these items refer to most conventional, store-bought versions, not homemade, whole-food versions.

- White sugar, brown sugar, high fructose corn syrup
- Soda pop, boxed and bottled juice, sports drinks, energy drinks
- Refined (white) flour and pasta
- Artificial sweeteners, colors, flavors, and preservatives
- Refined white table salt
- Margarine, most shortening (see substitute list in later chapter)
- Vegetable and canola oil
- Packaged foods labeled "low fat" or "fat free"
- Factory confined/raised meat, dairy, and eggs
- Processed meats
- Store bought ice cream
- Protein, energy, and granola bars
- Fast food / fried food
- Potato chips, crackers, pretzels, etc.
- Candy
- Cookies
- Fruit snacks
- Boxed cereal

Now, if you just can't bring yourself to do any more than remove THREE things from your diet, these are the three things I would recommend:

- Refined / processed sugar (white, brown, high fructose corn syrup)
- Refined / white processed foods (flour, pasta, salt)
- Artificial ingredients (sweeteners, colors, flavors, and preservatives)

If you're still feeling like you're going to have a nervous breakdown and can only remove ONE thing right now, then get rid of the sugar. Giving up sugar does not mean you have to give up sweets. You just have to know what to use and how to use it. Keep reading!

"To a significant degree, we are an overfed and undernourished nation digging an early grave with our teeth, and lacking the energy that could be ours." – Ezra Taft Benson

TOXIC SWEETENERS
(What You May Not Know)

ASPARTAME

This is a toxic chemical concoction, also known as Neotame (aka "aspartame on steroids"), NutraSweet, Equal, Spoonful, Canderel, E951, and Equal-Measure. It is made up of three chemical components: Aspartic acid, Phenylalanine, and Methanol. Aspartame is used in approximately 6,000 food products including:

- Diet soft drinks
- Juice
- Gum
- Candy
- Yogurt
- Milk
- Cereal
- Toothpaste
- Supplements
- Medications
- Ice cream
- Jello
- Hot chocolate
- Condiments
- Packaged / processed foods and snacks

Aspartame accounts for over 75% of adverse reactions to food additives reported to the FDA, including seizures and death. And yet it is still fully approved by the FDA, who claims it is safe. Look at this list of <u>documented</u> adverse reactions and chronic illnesses:

"Headaches/migraines, dizziness, seizures, nausea, numbness, muscle spasms, weight gain, rashes, depression, fatigue, irritability,

tachycardia, insomnia, vision problems, hearing loss, heart palpitations, breathing difficulties, anxiety attacks, slurred speech, loss of taste, tinnitus, vertigo, memory loss, joint pain, tumors, multiple sclerosis, epilepsy, chronic fatigue, Parkinson's disease, Alzheimer's, mental retardation, lymphoma, birth defects, fibromyalgia, and diabetes." – FDA.gov

HIGH FRUCTOSE CORN SYRUP / CORN SYRUP / CORN SUGAR

A monster-refined, cornstarch-derived product that is cheap and easily available, thanks to the government subsidy of the super-sized GMO corn industry. HFCS is linked to fatty liver disease and a myriad of other health conditions.

Note: HFCS has sought to re-brand itself now as "corn sugar." So if you see "corn sugar" on a label, don't get too excited. It's still the same junk.

WHITE SUGAR

Well, we all use it, right? (I used to, too; but not anymore.) Basically, they've taken the botanical grass/cereal grain known as sugar cane, and/or the cultivated plant "beta vulgaris" (sugar beet), and stripped them of every nutrient and mineral that ever existed in its natural form. (Not to mention the fact that most sugar beets are now GMO.)

Once it's passed the refining stage, it is chemically processed to create the white substance you buy at the grocery store. "Way back when," people used to chew on pure sugar cane. It not only strengthened their teeth, but it was also full of nutrients and actually nourished their teeth!

Here are the chemicals used in the sugar-refining process: Sulfur dioxide, Phosphoric acid, and Calcium hydroxide.

BROWN SUGAR

White sugar mixed with a little molasses. Still refined. Still chemically processed. Still toxic.

AGAVE

Such a controversial sweetener. Do you use it? I <u>used</u> to think that – as long as it was raw, organic, and unprocessed – it could be considered a healthy sweetener. I read all kinds of articles that disputed each other, and I continued to stick by my conclusion. All of that changed when I read a post written by my fellow "real food" friend, Angie Christensen (which can be found at *Simply Divine Eating*). It's all about the fructose. In short, we <u>don't</u> use it in 99% of our recipes anymore. I'll let you draw your own conclusions.

WHOLESOME SWEETENERS
(See, giving up processed sweeteners does not leave you without options!)

STEVIA

This is a zero calorie, non-glycemic sweetener that is actually an herb. The **green stevia plant** is pure and unrefined. I grow it myself, and it's fun! Just dry it and throw it in a small blender or coffee grinder to powder. A tiny amount goes a long way. On average, it's 300 times sweeter than sugar! Using too much can sometimes leave a funny aftertaste, so don't use too much.

White powder stevia and stevia extract have been processed. It's considered a safer sweetener than white sugar. I use it on occasion but not very often. Some brands still contain sugar and other chemical ingredients, so read the labels. If you're going for 100% whole food, choose the pure green herb itself.

COCONUT PALM SUGAR

The juice is extracted from the blossom of the coconut palm tree. It is simply the crystallized form of the juice. It is full of nutrients but is also high in fructose, which is toxic to the liver in high amounts. Like all sweeteners, don't use too much, too often.

Look for 100% organic, sustainable, unprocessed, and unbleached brands. This is a great sweetener for those who are converting to the 100% whole food lifestyle.

RAW HONEY

Use strained (not heavily filtered), local honey whenever possible! Raw honey is full of nutrients, if it has not been processed and the pollen is still present. It has been used throughout history medicinally for healing, internally and externally. Real raw honey never expires. It is anti-bacterial, anti-viral, and anti-fungal. Mixed with lemon juice, Ceylon cinnamon, warm water, and a pinch of cayenne pepper, it is excellent for coughs and sore throats. Raw honey can heal wounds, help combat allergies, and it is surprisingly beneficial for diabetics.

Approximately 70% of grocery store honey is not real honey. It's highly processed and often contains added ingredients, such as corn syrup, that aren't listed on the label. Store honey tastes NOTHING like fresh, raw honey.

100% MAPLE SYRUP

Straight from the tree is best! Real maple syrup is simply the sap from a maple tree and can be used for A LOT more than just pancakes and waffles. It is a great substitute for sweeteners in many desserts, treats, smoothies, and drinks. Pure unprocessed maple syrup also has nutrients still in tact, unlike the highly processed imitation maple syrup that is used in most homes today.

MOLASSES (BLACK STRAP, UNSULFURED)

This is made from the juices of sugar cane, sugar beets, or grapes. It's boiled down to a thick syrup by-product and still contains nutrients like magnesium, iron, potassium, and calcium. Blackstrap molasses is un-sulphured, which means it doesn't contain processed chemicals and is made from organic sugar cane.

DATES / DATE SUGAR

You can choose dehydrated and powdered dates (which are sometimes coated in oat flour).

EVAPORATED CANE JUICE

This is crystalized juice from the sugar cane. Organic is best.
It's still processed and not really healthy, but it's somewhat better than white sugar.

RAPIDURA/SUCANAT

This sweetener is sometimes processed, sometimes not. Read the labels and look at the color. It should be opaque and not look like crystals. It should look like little tiny, rough, tan-colored rocks, similar in appearance to coconut palm sugar. Be aware that it is still sugar. Eat sparingly.

XYLITOL

Another somewhat controversial sweetener, Xylitol is a sugar alcohol.
It actually helps prevent cavities and is an excellent aid in healing respiratory ailments. (Personal experience here!) Xylitol is derived from the birch tree or corn. I don't use it much in cooking anymore, because it is somewhat processed. If you do choose to use it, always purchase organic if it's corn-derived so you're not consuming GMO's.

Note: Xylitol is HIGHLY poisonous to dogs! Why dogs, but not other animals? I don't know. But please do not leave xylitol or foods made with it where your dogs could reach it!

GRAIN SWEETENERS

Wheat berries, whole barley, rye, brown rice, and oats can all be germinated and the sprouts used to sweeten bread dough or malted (roasted) for additional flavor when added to muffin, cookie, and cake batters. Soft winter wheat or pastry wheat yield a very sweet product. Be careful when purchasing pre-packaged grain sweeteners. That's a whole 'nuther story. Some are okay; but if you can make them at home, you're better off. Mother Earth News offers more information on that.

SALT

TABLE SALT / WHITE SALT – The Bad Stuff

Table salt is **97.5%** sodium chloride and **2.5%** chemicals and synthetic iodine. It is created by taking natural, unrefined salt (and sometimes crude oil extracts), and cooking it at 1200° Fahrenheit. Part of the salt processing includes the use of aluminum, ferrocyanide, and bleach. Synthetic iodine is then added back in.

Does this sound natural to you?

It's common for doctors to tell their sick patients to stop eating salt. Gee, I wonder why! (**Hint:** Because they're eating the wrong kind.)

Effects of white table salt:

- Swelling
- High blood pressure
- Kidney, thyroid, and liver problems
- Goiters
- Hypertension
- Heart disease
- Stroke
- Heart failure
- Nervous system disorders (anxiety/depression)
- Diabetes
- Obesity
- Muscle cramps
- Lymphatic system disorders

REAL SALT - The good stuff!

Natural salt is 100% necessary. We need it for:

- Good bone density
- Proper circulation
- Stabilized blood sugar levels
- Proper immune function
- Proper thyroid function
- Proper adrenal function
- Sufficient electrolytes
- Digestive enzymes (so we can assimilate nutrients from our food)

Pink Himalayan salt contains 84 minerals (including iodine) that are ESSENTIAL to our health. This is what I use 99% of the time. I've also used **Real Salt** brand of salt from Utah, **Celtic Sea Salt**, and **French Gray Salt**. I love them all. *San Francisco Salt Company* is my favorite resource for good salt. I purchase it in 10+ pound bags, and they even have different textures to choose from, such as coarse, medium, fine, and extra fine.

Once you convert to unrefined salt, you'll agree that white table salt tastes disgusting. Even the kids will agree. I promise! I even carry my own little container of pink salt in my purse for the rare occasion we eat at restaurants, and my kids ask me if they can use it. We all hate white table salt.

Note: If a pure white salt says "sea salt," it is not pure sea salt. It has still been processed. Un-processed salts have some kind of color and are not pure white. Don't be fooled by misleading labels and advertising!

GRAINS

Did you know that approximately HALF of Americans purposefully don't eat ANY whole grains? That is simply mind-blowing to me. Have we really lost our ability to educate ourselves about food? I've actually heard people say they didn't know that white flour comes from wheat. (And Jennifer shakes her head as she slowly walks away in disbelief.)

Whole grains are known as the "staff of life" for their historical importance to human survival. Also called "cereals," grains are the seeds of grasses, which are cultivated for food. (Not the same "cereal" you get in a cardboard box from the super market, which is HIGHLY processed, by the way.)

If a label just says, "whole grain" or "made with whole grain," then it still probably has refined and enriched white junk in it. Whole grains should always be listed first in the ingredients list and say "100% whole grain." This goes for bread, noodles, and any food product with grains. (Even when it does say "100% whole grain," it's still imperative to read the whole list for other possible unhealthy ingredients.) White flour/pasta is NOT healthy. It lacks vital nutrients, has synthetic vitamins added back in, and drives blood sugars sky high.

Whole grains will cook faster if you soak them first. I soak mine overnight, when I remember to do it. I also like to cook bigger batches and keep them in glass jars in the fridge for quick use. This way I can warm it up with a little water or broth for adding to a meal; or I can toss it on top of salads, yogurt, cereal, in a sandwich, or on top of soup!

Soaking (and sprouting) whole grains before using them is ALWAYS healthier. It breaks down phytic-acid, which binds to the nutrients and prevents them from being absorbed into the body. Soaking also helps pre-digest the grain and neutralizes enzyme inhibitors, which is highly beneficial, since grains are often difficult for the digestive system to break down. (This is very helpful for anyone who has digestive problems such as gluten intolerance or IBS.) Soaking/sprouting your grains also increases vitamin and mineral content. This is the same for nuts & seeds as well.

Cooking whole grains is as easy as cooking rice! On the *Whole Grains Council* website, there is a great chart that tells you exactly how long to cook each one of them.

Note: I know that there are a lot of people who are gluten free for one reason or another these days. This book does not specifically address that issue for a couple of reasons (and just as a side note, I do not personally believe in going 100% grain-free unless you are on a specific healing diet), but there are gluten-free grains available for intolerant people. Many gluten intolerant people can reverse the intolerance. They just don't know they can.

Also, I cook whole grain pasta longer than what the package says. Usually close to twice as long but at a lower temperature. Cooked this way, it's hard to tell the difference between white noodles and whole grain noodles.

TYPES OF GRAINS:

- Einkorn Wheat *(the most ancient and purest form of all wheat)*
- Hard Red Wheat
- Hard White Wheat
- Soft Wheat *(best for pastries, cookies, and cakes)*
- Brown Rice
- Wild Rice
- Barley
- Oats
- Corn / Popcorn
- Rye
- Kamut
- Spelt
- Farro
- Buckwheat
- Triticale
- Amaranth
- Teff
- Millet
- Sorghum
- Quinoa

NATURAL YEAST

*"One hears the occasional statement that milk makes mucous and
the saying is passed around from one uninformed person to another.
It may do so for a poorly nourished person, (or it may seem to do so).
There are people who can't eat wheat in any form - or strawberries
make their eyes swell, or produces hives, etc. Should it therefore be
said that strawberries make the eyes swell - or wheat gives one hives
and therefore no one should eat them? IF ONE IS COMPLETELY
NOURISHED, NO NATURAL FOOD WILL CAUSE THESE ILL
EFFECTS."* – John A. Widtsoe, Scientist

In the last few years, experts and laypersons alike have argued tooth and
nail about whether grain (particularly wheat) is good or bad. Many people are
going wheat free in their diets. Others are going gluten free. And yet others
are giving up grains completely! WHY? Haven't wheat and other grains been
eaten throughout history without any issues? Read on.

Wheat (grain) is referred to in the Bible as the Staff of Life. What is a staff?
It bears you up and supports you. Historically, wheat and grain have been
a main staple in the human diet. It's mentioned over and over throughout
scripture in various settings.

There are a number of reasons people are having issues with grains (particularly gluten grains, mainly wheat). One of those reasons is that modern
wheat has been severely hybridized, and our bellies are not handling it in a
friendly fashion. Einkorn wheat is the most ancient form of wheat in existence today. It's man's first form of cultivated wheat. It's a lot smaller than
modern wheat and looks a bit different, almost like a cross between wheat
and flat brown rice. It's classified as a "diploid," because it only has two sets
of chromosomes. Contrast that with the fact that 95% of modern wheat is
classified as a "hexaploid," because it has six sets of chromosomes due to all
the hybridization. Sigh. Frustrating, isn't it? Remind me again why they can't
just leave our food alone?

In ancient times, grains naturally sprouted themselves, as they were left in
the fields under the warm sun until they could be gathered up. (They didn't

have machinery to gather it quickly like we do now.) This process automatically broke down the anti-nutrients (natural preservatives) in grains. These natural preservatives have allowed wheat to stay good for thousands of years. They have even found wheat in ancient tombs that could still be sprouted.

Modern wheat (hard white, etc.) will at least be more easily tolerated, if you can just soak and/or sprout it first. But if you can afford it, Einkorn and other more ancient forms of wheat (such as Kamut and Spelt) are definitely the better choice.

Natural yeast (also called Pioneer Yeast or Natural Leavening) is where I'm heading now. It can be used for making regular homemade breads as well as sweet bread, waffles, pancakes, cinnamon rolls, muffins, donuts, and more. It is not always sour dough. This natural yeast is the yeast that has been historically used since the beginning of bread making. It is liquidy and bubbly, not dry and grainy like "store yeast."

Commercial yeast used today IS NOT NATURAL. "Modern" yeast was created in a laboratory in 1984 (possibly sooner, according to what Caleb Warnock, co-author of *The Art of Baking with Natural Yeast*, has since found out.) Our digestive systems don't recognize it, and some people are now allergic to the yeast itself! This is one of the several reasons for the rapid growth of Celiac disease, gluten intolerance/allergies, acid reflux, IBS, diabetes, skin issues, and more. Another problem is that commercial yeast is an isolated form of yeast that rises bread quickly but does not break down the gluten, phytic acid, and other anti-nutrients.

Natural yeast begins the digestion process before the grain ever even hits your mouth. It breaks down the harmful anti-nutrients (natural preservatives, such as phytic acid) ahead of time and turns it into a cancer-fighting antioxidant! Natural yeast "eats gluten." According to Caleb Warnock, it breaks the gluten chains down into amino acids! It will not spike blood sugar levels; it actually lowers them. (We know this from personal experience.) It's a pre-biotic AND pro-biotic. It helps your body to absorb vitamins, minerals, and fiber. It fights weight gain (doesn't cause it!), is good for your digestive system, and often times is very healing. Many people with wheat/gluten intolerances have been able to actually eat bread and gluten foods when using natural yeast! But the best part about natural yeast is that it can prevent these issues from happening in the first place. You can read more about this on Caleb's blog.

Some natural yeasts are very sour, some are a little sour, and some aren't sour at all. The best strains have been passed down for generations. Caleb offers a free sample of a 200-year-old strain of natural yeast flakes on his website, as well as instructions on how to activate and use it. When you grow your own natural yeast, you will NEVER have to buy yeast again. It is one of the most valuable preparedness foods you can store. You can even dehydrate or freeze it, and it will not die! I also highly recommend his beautiful book on baking with natural yeast. It is AMAZING.

Many "real food" bloggers and websites teach about soaking and sprouting grains, seeds, and nuts. I've also talked about it on my websites and often do it myself. This process also breaks down phytic acid and other anti-nutrients. My choice, though, when it comes to recipes that use yeast, is to not necessarily worry about soaking/sprouting *if I don't have time*, but to use natural "Pioneer" yeast instead. For more information, please visit the three best websites out there:

- Caleb Warnock's website
- Melissa Richardson's website, The Bread Geek
- Natural Leavening's website

There is hope, people! Grains (and wheat) in my opinion do not need to be (and <u>SHOULD NOT BE</u>) banished from the human diet. This is yet another modern fad, and gluten intolerance is a very sad health condition that should never have become an issue in the first place. Grains are a beautiful, natural, God-given food that are extremely healthful. What is detrimental to us are modern versions of overly-hybridized wheat, modern commercial yeast, "coming to America in the near future GMO wheat," improper grain preparation, refining, and processing. Because of these things and a few other contributing factors, most people in the U.S. now suffer from sickened guts (otherwise known as leaky gut syndrome and candida or systemic yeast over-growth). For more information about candida and how to heal it, see natural health educator Amy Jones's article at http://mindbodyandsoleonline.com/health-nutrition/taming-the-yeastie-beasties/.

Most of the bread recipes in this book do use commercial yeast. I occasionally use SAF brand. You can replace it with natural yeast in a recipe, if you know or learn how to do it. Because most people don't use or even know how to use natural yeast, I'm sharing basic recipes without natural yeast in this particular setting. To learn how to replace commercial yeast to natural yeast, please refer to Caleb's book and website mentioned above. He has said in one of the classes I took from him that when he regularly eats natural yeast throughout the week, he's also able to eat "junk" bread/ yeast without any problems, because his gut is strong. Even two or three times of making pancakes or scones with natural yeast each week will be better than none at all, and your digestive issues will improve dramatically.

FATS AND OILS

"The low-fat diet craze became popular in the 1970s after engineer Nathan Pritikin appeared on "60 Minutes" touting the success of his dietary approach. Pritikin was diagnosed with heart disease at a young age, and decided to change his diet. His theory, later labeled the "lipid hypothesis," claims that dietary fat, especially saturated fats and fats high in cholesterol, are to blame for America's No. 1 killer, heart disease. In the subsequent years, however, his hypothesis has come under greater scrutiny, and more research has been done on the important role of certain fats in the diet." – http://www.ehow.com/about_5344602_ dangers-low-fat-diet.html

We don't use a ton of fat. I don't believe a HIGH fat diet is healthy. However, fats are needed in our diets. They help our bodies absorb nutrients from the foods we do eat. We use oils and fats as long as they are un-processed, un-refined, cold pressed, and non-GMO.

Please, PLEASE stop using commercially-packaged foods labeled **"Low Fat."** They are SO unhealthy. They're processed (often hydrogenated, which is terrible); and they have added sugar, artificial sweeteners, and other toxic additives. They don't taste good (there's a reason for that), and they have a weird texture! It's not real food and should not be consumed by anyone. The oils you use should be unrefined, unprocessed, cold pressed, non-hydroge-nated, and organic if possible. Expeller pressed oils are not even very healthy. Although I do use them on occasion, I try to stay away from them most of the time. Here is a good article on expeller pressed oils (http://blog.fooducate.com/2010/12/08/what-is-expeller-pressed-oil-and-why-does-it-matter/).

Here is a list of oils and fats we use:

- Coconut oil (unrefined, cold pressed)
- Butter or ghee (from grass-fed cows)
- Extra virgin olive oil (unrefined, first cold pressed)
- Organic NON-hydrogenated cold-pressed shortening (Spectrum or Nutiva)
- Cold-pressed organic oils such as flax seed oil, almond oil, avocado oil
- Any produce and nuts such as avocados, walnuts, cashews, etc.

"Like so many of my patients, for years I tried one low-fat, low-cholesterol diet after another. But after failing to lose weight — and feeling pretty bad despite my "healthy diet" — I did a panel of blood tests on myself. The results were shocking. That fateful day was 25 years ago. It began my personal search for the truth about cholesterol and fat. What I learned at first surprised me, but now makes perfect sense. And I've proven it all in practice, both personally and with thousands of patients." – Marcelle Pick, OB/GYN NP, Women To Women

Here is a good article on choosing cooking oils, the myths and realities (http://www.ncbi.nlm.nih.gov/pubmed/10063298). And in this article, a world-renowned heart surgeon, Dr. Dwight Lundell, admits that he was wrong about fats being bad and why (http://preventdisease.com/news/12/030112_World-Renown-Heart-Surgeon-Speaks-Out-On-What-Really-Causes-Heart-Disease.shtml).

ANIMAL FOODS

Here are more of my thoughts on animal foods. My family has cut down significantly on them, especially meat and milk (as explained earlier in the book).

Our guts feel better when we don't eat a lot of meat. It doesn't digest as easily as other foods, and over time it putrefies in your intestines, causing build up. It's also very acidic. We do still eat meat once in a great while, but we have cut down on all animal foods a good 90%. When we do eat meat, we buy ONLY organic meat from grass-fed, pasture-raised, well-cared-for, humanely-treated animals, and we won't budge on that. We make sure to bless it at mealtime and express gratitude to God for allowing the animal to fulfill its measure of creation by feeding us.

We do not eat factory-confined / raised meats, dairy, or eggs. We buy raw milk, delivered from a small family farm that has been certified to sell their fresh milk. We buy eggs from local people who raise chickens on organic, non-GMO feed. And if I am not able to make homemade butter, sour cream, cheese, or yogurt, we purchase the best we can find at the time, organic and from farms when possible. Don't forget the Farmer's Markets. They're a great resource for buying farm fresh foods, both plant- and animal-based!

If you live in an area where you can't get fresh farm milk and pasture-raised animal foods, do your best to purchase organic from the grocery store. It's not perfect, but it ensures less pesticides and chemicals, and you won't have to worry about GMO's, as they are not allowed in organic foods (yet).

Our local Fred Meyer store carries grass-fed, organic, non-GMO milk that has been pasteurized. It's a "step up" alternative from conventional factory milk, and you know you're not getting a bunch of junk. I am not a fan of pasteurization or homogenization, however. Pasteurization kills nutrients and beneficial enzymes, and homogenization is actually toxic. Ultra-pasteurization is the WORST. *If* you are going to purchase something that's pasteurized, just make sure it is organic and not ultra-pasteurized.

Interesting to note, when we previously consumed pasteurized and/or homogenized dairy, it caused congestion and other issues. Since we have switched to farm fresh dairy, it causes no issues with congestion, and we can even have it when we're sick with respiratory illnesses, with no adverse effects. My daughter had food allergies and asthma for years, and they went away when we began using farm fresh milk. We also enjoy purchasing raw goat's milk, which is said to be more nutritious than dairy milk. If you're interested in knowing more about raw milk, you can read more about it on my "other" website, *The Modern Pioneer Mom.*

BEANS

Commonly Used Beans:

- Kidney
- Great Northern White
- Black
- Garbanzo (Chick Peas)
- Pinto
- Lentils
- Black Eyed Peas
- Lima
- Mung (awesome for sprouting)

Beans are often 1/4 the cost of cheese and 1/8 the cost of meat.

Because of the refined and processed junk that society has gotten used to eating, our bodies don't have the enzymes needed to properly digest high fiber beans and whole grains. Yeast imbalance may be the culprit, and gut healing may be in order. Once your gut is healed, the more whole foods you will eat, the more your body will build enzymes, and tummy trouble will be a thing of the past. Refer to the information on healing the gut in the previous "Natural Yeast" section.

Did you know that most beans take on the flavor of whatever you're cooking? They usually have very little taste, so you can use them in savory dishes OR sweet dishes.

Fresh is best, but if you are using canned beans, ALWAYS drain them first (except in the case of chili beans because you will need the flavored sauce).

Canned beans are very convenient. However, dry beans are much healthier and cheaper. I do use organic canned beans once in a while, but when time allows, I soak, over night, and cook up a big batch of bulk beans and freeze them for later use. I also sometimes dehydrate my cooked beans for convenient "instant" beans in future recipes.

Note: Most canned foods contain a chemical called BPA (Bisphenol - A) that disrupts the endocrine system and has been linked to numerous health conditions. It's best to keep commercially-canned foods to a minimum. There are some companies now offering "BPA FREE" cans, which is a better alternative; although some of them have been replaced with BPS, which is no better. Home canning in glass jars is a safer and healthier alternative.

IF BEANS ARE OLD, do not throw them out! You can always grind them into bean flour, which can be used in soups, baking, bread, etc. Another option is to pressure cook/can old beans, which should soften them right up. As with almost any food, the older they are, the less nutritious they are. However, these are good options if you don't want to waste your beans.

OPTIONS FOR USING BEANS:

- **Bean flour:** use for soups, thickener, sauces, gravies, and even baking! Mix bean flour with cold water first, stir, then add to hot liquid food. It only takes three minutes to fully cook bean flour!

  Note: Bean flour can be used in any recipe calling for flour by replacing up to 25% of wheat flour. Small white (Great Northern) beans are generally best for flour due to their milder taste.

  Example:
  Recipe calling for 4 c. wheat flour = 3 c. wheat flour and 1 c. bean flour

- **Mashed:** cooked or canned – use for meat substitute, dip, burritos, casseroles, baking, etc.
- **Frozen:** cooked, use whole or can be mashed
- **Sprouted:** use in most recipes just like cooked beans, or use on salads, in sandwiches, etc.

Chapter 7

Make it Real! Convert Your Fake Food Recipes

I t's easy to convert fake food recipes to real food recipes. When substituting, you can use whatever whole food version of that ingredient you want. For instance, if a recipe calls for milk, you can choose cow, goat, almond, oat, soy, chia, flax, etc. (The only one you may want to be careful with is coconut milk because it is much thicker and sometimes has a stronger taste. Just experiment.)

Let me let you in on a little secret.

I have rarely been able to find a good recipe online that is labeled "healthy" and actually tastes good. If I search "healthy banana bread recipe," or "healthy brownie recipe," it usually doesn't make the cut, at least for me. The texture is weird, or the taste is just BLEGH. And I don't go for BLEGH. I am HUGE on flavor and texture!

Make herbs and spices your best friend! Learn how to use them. It's not hard! Also, use a good unrefined salt (such as Pink Himalayan salt or RealSalt®) and fresh ground pepper. If a savory food still needs more "kick," add a pinch or two of celery seed. You'll be amazed at what that little tip can do for your food. For sweet recipes, I promise you'll get to the point where you don't want your food as sweet as you do now. If you feel like you need more sweetener, add a tiny amount of Stevia. Start small and add more if you need it. A little goes a long way.

Convert your junk food recipe. Don't be afraid. Nine times out of 10, it will be much better than any online "healthy" version. Now granted, I have yet to be able to recreate the perfect white cake or white buttercream or royal frosting. I've let go of the need, but I'm keeping it in the back of my subconscious mind just in case. For anything that's not pure white (other than my homemade marshmallow recipe), just substitute the junk ingredients for real food ingredients and accept the beautiful hint of color.

Example:

1 c. white sugar + 1 c. brown sugar = 2 c. coconut palm sugar

2 c. white flour = 1 ¾ c. whole wheat flour

½ c. agave = ½ c. raw honey or 100% maple syrup

½ c. margarine = ½ c. real butter or coconut oil

Note: Whole-wheat flour absorbs moisture faster, so you will want to use just a tiny bit less than the white flour the recipe would call for. Estimate. You usually don't have to be exact.

Below are a few helpful substitutions. (You'll find more as you learn real food.) Some of these are fake food to real food substitutions, and some of them are just real food alternatives you're welcome to use, depending on your preferences.

Note: My recipes don't really cater to specific diets other than real whole food. I don't purposefully leave out wheat, beans, dairy, corn, etc., from my recipes. If you need to adjust a recipe to meet your specific needs, go for it! Below you will find some common food substitutions. You may or may not need to substitute; just experiment and see what you like. You might find that as you play with recipes, you'll like your version even better! It happens to me all the time. I improve other people's recipes A LOT. It's super fun!

Original

Substitution

- Butter / Margarine

- Coconut oil, extra virgin olive oil

- White Flour

- Whole wheat or spelt flour

Make it Real! Convert Your Fake Food Recipes

Original	Substitution
• White / brown sugar	• Coconut palm sugar
• White noodles	• 100% Whole grain noodles
• White rice	• Brown rice or wild rice
• White table salt	• Pink Himalayan or Real Salt®
• Syrup (of any kind)	• 100% Maple syrup, raw honey, homemade fruit sauce
• Chicken / beef broth	• Vegetable broth
• Pecans / walnuts	• Almonds or cashews
• Peanut butter	• Almond or other nut butter
• Cow's milk	• Goat, almond, soy, coconut, rice milk
• Canola / vegetable oil	• Olive oil, coconut oil, avocado oil, etc.
• Buttermilk	• Plain kefir
• White / apple cider vinegar	• Raw unfiltered apple cider vinegar
• Mayonnaise	• Homemade mayo or healthy, organic, non-GMO mayo
• Soy sauce	• Braggs liquid aminos or organic, non-GMO soy sauce
• Corn starch	• Arrowroot powder or organic corn starch

A note about the recipes in this book AND every single other recipe you ever experiment with. (Did you notice the word **experiment**?) If you make a recipe and don't like it, don't automatically tag it as a bad recipe! I've taken several recipes that turned out rather . . . well . . . un-edible, and turned them into something wonderful that my family loves.

A few of my recipes say "A little of this and a little of that." This is because that's literally how you make them; and by labeling them as such, you have fair warning. How exciting is that! I call them, "Jennifer Make Up the Recipes." Again, experiment. Toss in whatever amount looks good to you, taste, adjust, and make them your own. The more you do this, the better you'll get at it.

Recipes are meant to be played with. That's a rule I made up and 100% believe in. I'm giving you permission to change the ingredients and make it your own. I nearly guarantee you'll like most, if not all, of the recipes here; but if you have issues with any of them, don't give up. Turn it into a science lab class and see what you can create! If there really is a huge problem with a recipe, please go to my website and use the contact page to tell me what the problem is. I'll be happy to help you fix it.

Chapter 8

The Well-Stocked Pantry

elow is the list many people have asked me for: my pantry list. It's definitely not exhaustive, but it's a great reference for you to keep close as you begin to fill your kitchen with real, whole, nourishing foods. You may find that you'll add to it, as I'm sure I have accidentally left some foods out. However, these are the general foods that I try to keep on hand on a regular basis. This list will be expanded in my R.E.A.L. online course. In the course, I will also teach you how to create what's called the **Home Grocery Store**. You will learn how to have a set-up in not only your kitchen but also your home, one that is organized, well-stocked, and replenish-able without having to go on full grocery excursions every single week. For now, let's work on getting you familiar with just a few of the foods that are most often found in a real food kitchen:

- Whole grains
- Flour and rolled grains
- Whole grain pasta
- Beans / Legumes
- Raw nuts and seeds
- Healthy fats and oils
- Pink Himalayan Salt or REAL© Salt
- Braggs Liquid Aminos (non-GMO soy sauce)
- Braggs raw un-filtered apple cider
- Nutritional Yeast
- Spirulina (If you're not sure what that is, you can "Google" it)
- Homemade stock (vegetable or animal based)

- Fresh and dehydrated herbs and spices
- Natural food colorings / flavorings (avoid artificial ingredients!)
- Real vanilla and real vanilla beans
- Unsweetened coconut (flakes or shredded)
- Raw Cacao powder (or un-alkalized high quality cocoa powder)
- Carob powder
- Homemade or "Enjoy Life" brand mini chocolate chips
- Stevia (green stevia herb and some liquid extracts)
- Raw unfiltered honey
- Coconut palm sugar
- 100% Maple syrup - grade B (less processed)
- Molasses (un-sulfured) / Black Strap Molasses
- Fruits and Vegetables – Fresh / Frozen / Dehydrated
- Raw Milk / Kefir / Yogurt / Cheese / Sour Cream (farm fresh if possible)
- Farm Fresh Eggs
- Organic, cold pressed, non-hydrogenated shortening
- Sourdough / Natural Yeast / Homemade bread
- Homemade (or no-junk organic) Ketchup, Sauces, Salad Dressings
- Homemade (or no-junk organic) Jam / Jelly, Cream Of Soups, Mayo
- Homemade (or no-junk organic) Peanut butter / Almond butter
- Homemade (or no-junk organic) Granola
- Homemade (or no-junk organic) Tortillas and tortilla chips
- Homemade or Bubbies brand pickles / sauerkraut
- Homemade snacks (granola bars, cookies, crackers)

And don't forget about sprouts! One of the best sources of nutrition available is through sprouted foods. You can make wheat grass, and you can sprout grains, beans, and seeds very easily using a sprouter or even a canning jar. Sprouts are also easier to digest and provide a near-instant boost of energy. Some of the most popular sprouting seeds are alfalfa, clover, broccoli, wheat, and beans. You can easily find them online or at your local natural food store.

Chapter 9

Organize, Systemize, Utilize

*T*here are a million and ten ways to organize your real food life, and there's no way I could cover them all here in this book. It would take an entire book in itself to do that, but below are a few of my favorite ideas to help you get a good start now.

- **Glass canning jars** – These are my very #1 favorite pantry organizer of all time. Wide mouth, in my opinion, are the easiest to work with because you can fit your hand and large spoons and scoops in there to get stuff out. They fit on your pantry shelves, in your kitchen cabinets, in your refrigerator/freezer, and they're pretty out in the open. You can vacuum seal them with your jar attachment, if it's not something you use very often, and then the contents inside will last up to 10 times as long. I keep grains, beans, nuts, seeds, granola, noodles, coconut, chocolate/carob chips, baking staples, and more in my jars. Anything that fits!

- **Labeler** – "Label, label, label!" Invest in a labeler; your life will never be the same. I've been known to label nearly everything: jars, containers, bins, boxes, kitchen cabinet and pantry shelves, refrigerator / freezer shelves, the insides of drawers, and more. You'd think it's not necessary because you know your own kitchen. However, you don't realize how wonderful it is to have things labeled until after you label them. Your spouse, kids, and guests won't be asking where things go (or where things are) near as much, and you won't be so tempted to just throw things in the drawer or on a shelf because the labels will be staring you in the face. Once you start labeling, you will wonder why it took you so long to do it.

- **Bins** – This includes fabric bins, plastic bins, open bins, bins with lids, big bins, small bins, whatever kinds of bins appeal to you. These are perfect to store bulk herbs, herbal tea, smaller pantry items, kitchen tools, health care / medicinal items, cookie cutters, homemade oatmeal packets, snacks, etc. Use them in your pantry, cabinets, fridge, and freezer. (And don't forget to label them!)

- **Recipe Binder** – Instead of dealing with piles and piles of cookbooks on your counter or falling out of your cabinet, why not combine the recipes you like to use (your favorites as well as the ones you've been dying to try but haven't yet gotten around to making) in an organized binder? You can create sections just like a recipe book. Use page protectors, copy the recipes (or even rip the recipe out of the book if you need to), and slide them down into the page protectors. You can even make a table of contents. Easy peasy!

- **Menu Planner** – There are more menu planning methods than there are stars in the sky. Almost. Why menu plan anyway? It saves time, money, and sanity. You always know what you're going to eat ahead of time. No more "Mom! What's for dinner?" And better yet, no more standing in the kitchen with the deer in the headlights look on your face as you gaze into the pantry wondering what to fix, only to give up and tell your kids to pour a bowl of cereal. Yuck! You'll buy only what is on your list for your menu plan, and you won't have to search for ingredients anymore, or run to the store at the last minute, because you'll already have all the ingredients you need for your meals.

One of the simplest ways to menu plan is to use a blank calendar or sheet of paper divided into individual days. In each square/section write something like this:

Breakfast – Overnight Oatmeal
Lunch – Fruit and Kale Salad
Dinner – Burritos and Mexican Rice
Snacks – Herbed Popcorn

You can plan ahead for one week, two weeks, three weeks, four weeks, or even three months! Anitra Kerr of *Simply Living Smart* has a whopping 90-day menu plan! They only eat the same meal four times per year. Isn't that amazing? I tend to stick to the two-week meal plan most of the time, because it's easy. (Mine changes here and there because I'm constantly trying new recipes and testing new foods, so our preferences change; but we do have the timeless recipes that our family loves, and those tend to stay on the menu no matter what. This last couple of years I got out of the menu planning habit, and it left a weight on my shoulders. Menu planning makes life so much easier!)

Once you have a list of meals you want for the next two weeks (or however long you choose), make a list of the ingredients needed for each recipe. Estimate how much of each of those ingredients you'll need. If you're like me, you'll usually purchase a little (or a lot) extra, so you don't have to go back to the store as often. And it adds to your food storage supply and saves money to buy in bulk. Turn those ingredients into a grocery list, and you'll be set to go!

You may have to buy dairy, produce, etc. more often than your major menu-shopping trip, because they're a bit more perishable than some foods. It's okay. Just stick with whatever is on the list, and you'll be fine. Know that if you find an extra good deal, which usually only happens in a close-out event, and your bank account is okay with it, it's wise to purchase extra during the sale to save both money and time.

I have bulk foods stored in 5-gallon buckets and #10 cans. I use quart and ½ gallon glass canning jars as well as plastic bins to organize my pantry. I use smaller pint and quart jars to organize my cabinets. When my jars and bins run low, I replenish from my larger storage. I keep "like" foods with "like" foods. So on one shelf or section, I'll organize all my grains. In another section might be beans, pasta, oils, or snacks. I keep all my herbs and spices in like-sized, small jars in a drawer. I organize my refrigerator and freezer the same way: dairy on one shelf, vegetables on another, fruits on another, etc. These are all my grocery "aisles." When they run low, I replenish from my "stock room," which is essentially my buckets and #10 cans full of food or my bulk herbs and spices that I keep in the fridge or freezer. The goal is to build up your stock room (bulk) supply, so you don't have to go to the grocery store as often. This allows you to stay organized and have the convenience of your own Home Grocery Store!

The initial organizing and systemizing is the hardest part, if you can even call it "hard." (I call it fun!) **Remember, a mess usually has to be made first in order to get everything organized.** Do as I did. Pull everything out of your pantry and cupboards. Do the same thing with your fridge and freezer. Throw away "questionables" and junk food. Divide like items into groups and start containerizing, and then begin to fill your kitchen with more & more real foods, as you're able to. It's VERY empowering and satisfying to look at a kitchen full of beautiful, organized containers and then know exactly what to do with them, because you've planned your meals.

Chapter 10

But We Can't Afford to Eat Healthy

Really—You can't afford not to. Let's take a look at some perspective. Health care (or let's just call it what it really is: SICK CARE) costs this country billions of dollars each year, and our overall health is not improving. It's getting worse. An average visit to a doctor for typical ailments is anywhere from $100-$200. Surgeries and treatments cost thousands of dollars, sometimes more.

Depending on where you live, purchasing real food from the grocery store can cost an average of anywhere from 25%-50% more than what processed and packaged, fake foods cost. I'm certainly not the world's richest person, but it's still worth it to me and my family to give up other things that we may not need and adjust our budget to pay for good foods that give us a better chance of not having to go to the doctor. Why pay for junk that's going to cause more dis-ease risk and cost a lot more money in the long run? It may be a little more expensive in the short term, but looking at the long-term costs if I don't eat healthy is enough to send anyone to the loony bin. I know this first hand. It's EXPENSIVE to not be in good health.

Keeping a price book may be beneficial. This allows you to keep track of how much certain food items cost at each store, so you can track where the best deals are. Eventually you'll just remember that they "cost less here than over there." You can adjust your price book as item costs change, if needed.

That said, I'm going to give you some more resources for keeping real food "affordable." This is in addition to (obviously) cooking your food from scratch and avoiding pre-packaged foods, which ounce for ounce are astronomically priced and fail to satisfy or nourish anyone.

- **Gardening:** Very simply put, plant a garden. You can use a big plot of land, raised garden beds, or even a small back porch pot. Plant fruit trees, too. If you have kids, get them involved. Once you have an established garden with good topsoil, it's nearly FREE to produce your own food! Caleb Warnock teaches & has written a book about winter gardening also. You can garden year round and have fresh produce for your entire family at virtually no cost!

- **Farmer's Markets / Local Farms:** I could spend all day strolling around viewing all the beautiful produce, herbs, and natural products sold by these vendors. Most often the prices are extremely reasonable; and if you go later in the day, sometimes you'll luck out and be able to pay ½ price. I've gotten grocery sacks full of fruits and vegetables for $2-3 before! Many of these farmers offer organic, non-GMO foods and sometimes even raw milk, fresh eggs, and raw honey. I can't tell you how good it feels to come home with bags full of fresh foods from a Farmer's Market. If you've been to one, I'm sure you know what I mean.

- **Co-ops:** My favorite food co-op is Bountiful Baskets. They've gone nationwide and are available to most people in the U.S. now. They often provide in-season fruits, vegetables, and other foods at a fraction of the cost of grocery stores; and their pick up times are weekly. It's very affordable and convenient. Little House Living's website is a great resource for finding co-ops in your local area.

- **Warehouse Stores:** Costco. Need I say more? Gosh I love that store! There are other warehouse stores also, like Sam's Club & BJ's. If you have one anywhere near you, utilize it! It's a great way to save money in the long run by purchasing real food in bulk. And yes, they have a very nice selection of real food. Trader Joe's, WinCo, and Natural Grocers aren't exactly warehouse stores, but they are large and do carry a good selection of real food at less-than-typical "big city" or "small town" prices. Remember to check the ingredients list, as these stores do still carry a good bit of packaged, processed food that "claims" to be healthy but isn't really. I'm happy that our real food choices are growing in these places, though.

- **Online Stores:** Amazon Prime is wonderful! You can get almost anything you'd purchase at a brick-and-mortar store through Prime; and it's almost always cheaper. They also offer free 2-day shipping. Azure Standard, Thrive Market, and Vita-Cost offer great discounts on their food and natural products, too.

Ultimately, it would be best to buy 100% organic foods, or even better to grow and raise your own. The Environmental Working Group's website states this:

> *"Nearly two-thirds of the 3,015 produce samples tested by the U.S. Department of Agriculture in 2013 contained pesticide residues - a surprising finding in the face of soaring consumer demand for food without agricultural chemicals. EWG's Shopper's Guide to Pesticides in Produce calculates that USDA tests found a total 165 different pesticides on thousands of fruit and vegetables samples examined in 2013."*

Pretty astonishing numbers; and pretty supportive of the need to focus on organic eating. However, I know personally that sometimes change happens in stages. If you don't feel that you can afford to put out the extra money up-front for organic produce right now, you can at least take the "better" approach by purchasing the "Clean Fifteen" and avoiding the "Dirty Dozen," as explained on the EWG's website.

No matter which route you go for purchasing foods and natural household items, it helps to create a menu plan and stick to it. That way you're not purchasing more than what you planned on eating anyway. Coupons can sometimes be used on real food, but there honestly aren't that many out there. If you can find some and use them, go for it! I used to be the queen of couponing in my town. I had a 4" binder and taught classes locally and out of state, as well as for a military wives group. I saved all kinds of money by using coupons; but 90% of what I bought was junk, even though I didn't realize it then. When I figured out how to really take care of my health and transform my kitchen, I tossed that binder full of coupons in the trash and never looked back.

Chapter 11

Kitchen Gear

arage tools. They're usually high quality, so they last many years and do
the job right, correct? You're willing to pay a higher price for those items
and not skimp on cheap discount store tools, right? (If you're a mom/wife/
lady, I'm guessing your husband/dad/guy friends are the ones who take care
of this area. It is their domain, of course. Unless you're a female who lives in
the garage and stays out of the kitchen, which is probably rare.)

Why would your kitchen be any different? It's your domain. In my
opinion, I think the kitchen trumps the garage. **The kitchen is where you
prepare the very thing that keeps you alive.** The garage is not. I'm not
saying, "go get rid of your garage tools." What I am saying, though, is that
you deserve (your family deserves!) to have good, high-quality tools in your
kitchen that will do the job and last a very long time. Don't skimp on price
and quality. I promise, you'll regret it if you do.

We weren't able to purchase all of my kitchen tools at one time. I was
super happy to get a high-powered Blendtec® for Christmas, a WonderMill
wheat grinder for my birthday, and a Bosch mixer for my anniversary. This
was over the course of a couple of years as we saved for them. I slowly
stocked up on what I felt I could afford at the time; and, with a couple of
small "want, not need" exceptions, I now have nearly all the tools necessary
to make full use of my real food kitchen. Here is a good list of kitchen
tools I suggest you work toward getting, if you don't already have them.
This is in addition to the basics that most people usually receive at their
wedding reception (like four toasters, three can openers, and a pile of ugly
pot holders).

Helpful Real Food Kitchen Tools:
- Blendtec / Vitamix high powered blender

- Bosch mixer
  (for larger jobs like baking bread or shredding cooked chicken)
- Kitchen Aid mixer
  (for smaller jobs)
- Grain grinder
  (Wonder/Whisper Mill is my favorite and grinds beans and corn too)
- Food Processor
- Hand-held immersion blender
- Rice cooker
- Slow cooker
- Pressure cooker
  (optional)
- Mandoline slicer
- Popcorn air popper
- Sprouter
- Tortilla maker
- Nut chopper
- Grater and fine grater
  (for zest, cheese, etc.)
- Coffee grinder
  (for herbs, spices and seeds)
- High quality mixing bowls
  (preferably glass, ceramic, or stainless steel)
- Non-toxic pots and pans
  (stainless, cast iron, ceramic)
- Colander and fine mesh strainer
- Splatter guard for sauté pans
- Good quality cutting boards
  (stay away from plastic, if possible)
- Apple peeler-corer-slicer
- Salad spinner
- Herb scissors
- Kitchen shears and high quality knives
- Whisks of different sizes and types

Kitchen Gear

- Wood rolling pin
- Various sized baking pans
  (glass and stainless)
- Salad dressing / Sauce shakers
- Biscuit cutters
- Dough slicer
- Ice Cream maker
- Waffle iron
  (makes more than just waffles!)
- Food Saver / Vacuum Sealer
  (with jar attachments)
- Parchment paper
- Glass canning jars
  (tiny spice jar sizes all up to ½ gallon sizes)
- Spiralizer

Hopefully I didn't forget anything here, either!

Chapter 12

Conclusion

We tend to do important, life-changing things for two reasons: Desperation and inspiration. In my case, it was both. I was desperate to overcome the health challenges I had and wanted to be happier. I felt I had no other choice but to do the <u>opposite</u> of what I'd been doing for so many years.

If you're doing the same exact thing over and over, expecting to get different results, you're going to be very disappointed. Once I started making changes, inspiration came flooding in, and I couldn't help but want to make even more changes. It was exciting and much easier than I thought it would be. If you are desperate now, then the time is now. But if you're not desperate yet, then why wait until you BECOME desperate? Why not START NOW, and prevent future misery? Taking one step at a time is easy; and in this case, it can even be fun!

Holistic, healthy living isn't a modern fad with fading results. It's a historical way of life with permanent results. If you've never done anything like this, believe in yourself. You CAN do it! If you're already "into" real food somewhat, or even if you're a nearly 100% real food junkie like me, take the ideas and tips I give you in this book and raise your bar. Step your current system up a notch and see how you can make what you're already doing even better!

Maybe you follow other people's recipes but don't experiment with your own. Start experimenting! Maybe your kitchen is still a mess, even though you're eating the right things. Organize it! Maybe you're spending too much money on healthy pre-packaged store bought foods and need to learn how to cook at home from scratch. Pull out your pots and pans, order your natural yeast culture, and go soak some beans!

You can do this. I promise. If you'll dedicate yourself to making these changes, your life will improve. Food changes alone will result in your family being happier, getting sick less often, having more energy, and feeling better about yourselves!

If you're not someone who has fun in the kitchen right now, give yourself a chance. I'm confident that as you begin to discover real food and involve God in the process to help you, you will grow to love it! I'm excited for you to begin your journey to better health and happiness. Watch as you and your children transform, and your family's atmosphere becomes more peaceful, too.

Now just like I did, roll up your own sleeves, take this first of my three steps, and bless yourself and your family with a nourishing, R.E.A.L. food kitchen. Again, it's time to **Really Embrace Abundant Living!** Wouldn't you agree?

Chapter 13

Food Healing Testimonials

My husband used to have chronic stomach pain. We cut out processed foods, started eating green smoothies, and cut down on the meat. It went away. I didn't have any specific health problems, but I just didn't feel good or have energy. I thought, "If this is how I feel in my early twenties, what am I going to feel like when I get older"? I knew something was not right so I was ready to listen, when my friend started to teach me. When I mentioned how I was feeling and she asked what I was eating it was the first time that it really clicked for me that healthy food meant healthy bodies. My mom tried to teach me but I guess I needed a second witness!

- Heather Nebeker

I suffered with severe IBS for years and infertility. I had a blood test done by a holistic doctor and found out I was intolerant to gluten, dairy, eggs. I cut those foods out for one month. For the first time in years my stomach problems were gone and I got pregnant the next month. I can now eat those foods again with no problem. I just needed a break for a while to allow my gut to heal.

- Debbie Welch

My husband, since the age of three months, has been given sugar in his food at all times. He was so sugar driven, that when he finished with any food, he always needed a sweet treat. He's been overweight his entire life. I started teaching him that he didn't need the sugar afterwards, & that healthy fruit smoothies every morning would help. Since implementing that, he hasn't craved sugar in over a year!

- Christine Hall

My husband, Nathan, was having extreme stomach issues. We cut out friend food, pork, beans, & limited red meat. It changed everything! He also quit drinking soda, which helped his wrist heal after tearing all the ligaments.
- *Trisha Ganoe*

Drinking raw milk gets rid of heartburn for me & keeps me full longer. My husband has started adding fruits & vegetables to his diet & is eating home cooked meals more than eating out. In just 2 weeks there is a noticeable difference in his weight, & he has more energy.
- *Becky Dawson*

I thought I was having a gluten intolerance issue because of the intense stomach pain it caused. I switched to natural yeast, & I can now eat bread & pizza with no problem!
- *Diana Vigil*

The Recipes

Bread & Breakfast

PERFECTLY PERFECT WHOLE-WHEAT BREAD

4 c.	Hot water
	(hot to touch, but not burning)
½ c.	Coconut or olive oil
½ c.	Raw unfiltered honey or molasses
2 Tbsp.	SAF brand yeast
	(no yeast proofing needed)
2 Tbsp.	Raw unfiltered vinegar
	(like Braggs brand)
2 Tbsp.	Unrefined salt
	(I use Pink Himalayan)
1-2 c.	Rolled oats or steel cut oats
1-2 Tbsp.	Ground flax seed / chia seeds
	(optional but awesome -
	use either or combo)
Up to 12 cups	Fresh ground whole-wheat flour

*This recipe makes four 8" loaves or three 12" loaves
(I use Norpro dimpled bread pans).

INSTRUCTIONS

First, let me apologize ahead of time. I don't mean to yell at you in these instructions, but it's somewhat necessary. Please do not take it personally.

1. Combine hot water, yeast, oil, honey, and about 1 cup of flour and mix for a few seconds.
2. Add vinegar, salt, chia seeds, oats, and more flour
3. Keep adding flour just until the sides of the bowl start to clean themselves, and dough pulls away from edge. There should be NO flour sticking to the sides of the bowl after about 7 rotations or so. If there

is, add another ¼ c. flour at a time, until there's no more sticking. Let knead for 10-12 minutes.

4. Preheat oven to 125° F to 140° F (or as low as your oven will go).
5. TURN THE OVEN OFF. This pre-heating is ONLY for dough rising. If you don't turn it off, it will ruin your bread!
6. Turn off mixer. Cover your hands and the counter with coconut or olive oil. (Use oil, NOT FLOUR.)
7. Divide dough using a knife (don't pull dough apart) into 4 small or 3 large loaves. Flatten on counter, shape into dough loaves, then add loaves to pans. Can brush with egg and sprinkle oats over top of loaves for a more artisan look, if you choose.
8. Let pans sit in oven for 45-60 minutes to rise up to about ¼" below the sides of the pan. (MAKE SURE THE OVEN IS TURNED OFF)
9. When dough has risen, leave it alone. IN the oven. DO NOT open oven door. DO NOT be tempted to sniff or touch. DO NOT remove!
10. Turn the oven on to 350° F (no pre-heating). Bake for 32-35 minutes. Remove from pans, let cool, and store in bread bags.

*Note: Feel free to add cinnamon, raisins, sweetener, herbs, cheese, etc. to this recipe. Simply add whatever "add-ins" you'd like before dumping in all of the flour. After you have the amount of add-ins you want, then finish with the rest of the flour until the sides come clean.

EZEKIEL BREAD

Grind the following ingredients in wheat grinder:
(Use course setting; flour will still be very fine.)

5 c.	Dry wheat kernels
1 c.	Dry barley
¼ c.	Dry pinto beans
¼ c.	Dry soy beans (organic)
¼ c.	Dry lentils
1 c.	Rye
⅓ c.	Millet

Add the following to bread mixer:

5 c.	Warm water
3 Tbsp.	SAF yeast
¼ c.	Honey (raw, if possible)
¼ c.	Molasses (100% Grade B is best)
½ c.	Real butter softened, or coconut oil
2 Tbsp.	Unrefined salt
1 ½ - 2 Tbsp.	Lemon juice
1-2 Tbsp.	Raw unfiltered apple cider vinegar

INSTRUCTIONS

1. Knead well for 2-5 minutes, then add other half of flour mixture. Knead 8 minutes more (longer if kneading by hand).
2. Instructions are similar to the whole-wheat bread recipe. Divide dough (cut with knife) into 4 small or 3 large loaves and place in lightly greased bread pans.

3. Preheat oven to 125° F to 140° F. TURN OVEN OFF AFTER IT HEATS UP. Place loaves in preheated oven and let rise for 30-60 minutes. Temperature and humidity determine how long it takes to rise.

4. Leave loaves in the oven, turn on heat to 350° F, and let bake for 35 minutes.

PITA BREAD

2 c.	Hot water
2 tsp.	Raw honey or coconut palm sugar
1 Tbsp.	Unrefined salt
5+ c.	Whole-wheat flour
2 Tbsp.	SAF yeast
	(or equivalent of natural yeast – refer to Natural Yeast section for more info)

INSTRUCTIONS

1. Preheat pizza stone to 475° F. (Can also be cooked in a pan on the stovetop. This way it will be more like flat bread.)
2. Mix all ingredients and knead for 6-7 minutes. You may need to use more or less than 5 cups of flour, just add enough that it cleans the sides of the bowl. You don't want it too sticky to work with and shape/roll or too dry.
3. Roll into golf-ball-sized balls. Let rest for 10 minutes.
4. Roll with rolling pin to ¼" thick, and let rest for 10 more minutes. (Use coconut or olive oil instead of flour to keep dough from sticking to counter. Oil will keep the pitas softer.)
5. Bake on hot pizza stone for 4-7 minutes, turning over between 1 ½ minutes and 2 ½ minutes, depending on your oven. You don't want it to be crisp, just soft and pliable. So play around with your oven heat to figure out the right time for you. They will puff up into a ball in the oven.
6. Let cool on wire rack, and use sharp knife to cut open.

*Note: You may need to add more flour (and flour your surface/hands instead of oiling them).

BAGELS

¼ c.	Milk or water
1 Tbsp.	SAF yeast
1 Tbsp.	Raw honey
1 Tbsp.	Coconut or olive oil
1 tsp.	Unrefined salt
2 Tbsp.	Butter
1	Egg white
2½ c.	Whole-wheat flour

INSTRUCTIONS

1. Knead above ingredients until sides of bowl are clean.
2. Pour in ½ c. more water until dough is soft, smooth, and satiny, but not too sticky.
3. Mix another 30 seconds.
4. Place dough on lightly oiled surface. Let sit 15 minutes.
5. Divide into 12 pieces. Shape into balls.
6. Poke hole in middle with thumb and pull around edge until a bagel shape is made.
7. Placed on lightly greased baking sheet and let stand 15 minutes.
8. Bring to boil: 2 quarts water, 2 Tbsp. raw honey
9. Place 3-4 bagels at a time into boiling water. When they rise to the surface, turn them over and cook until puffy (about 2 minutes).
10. Remove and put back on cookie sheet. Brush tops of bagels with egg glaze (1 egg beaten with 2 Tbsp. cold water).
11. Bake at 425° F for 20-25 minutes or until golden brown. Cool on baking rack.

BAGEL VARIATIONS

Add any of these to the basic bagel dough recipe:

2 Tbsp.	Minced onions or onion powder
2 Tbsp.	Sunflower seeds
¼ c.	Fresh blueberries or other berries (cut into small pieces)
1-2 Tbsp.	Dill weed
¼ c.	Chopped spinach or other veggies
3 Tbsp.	Raisins or other dried fruit
1 ½ Tbsp.	Coconut palm sugar
1 tsp.	Cinnamon
¼ tsp.	Nutmeg
¼ - ½ c.	Raisins

PERFECTLY FLAKEY PIE CRUST

3 c.	Whole-wheat flour
1 tsp.	Unrefined salt
2 tsp.	Raw honey or coconut palm sugar
1 ½ c.	Organic, cold-pressed shortening
1	Egg
1 Tbsp.	Raw vinegar
⅓ c.	Icy COLD water

INSTRUCTIONS

1. Mix flour, salt, and sugar. Cut in shortening until crumbly. Add egg, water, and vinegar. Fold LIGHTLY but thoroughly with fingers.
2. Put in fridge for 20 minutes to chill dough. Take out and divide into three sections. (Unused sections go into the freezer.)
3. Roll out very thin, until almost transparent. It needs to be big enough to hang over edges of pie pan by 2-3 inches. Trim edges with knife or scissors to one inch past edge of pie pan.
4. Press flutes into edges with finger / thumb and poke holes in bottom of crust with fork.
5. Mold foil into a bowl shape to fit inside of crust. Lightly place inside of crust.
6. Bake at 400° F for 10 minutes or until light golden brown. Remove foil, let cool, and fill.

CINNAMON SUGAR

1-2 Tbsp.	Cinnamon
	(depending on personal preference)
1 c.	Coconut palm sugar

INSTRUCTIONS

Put ingredients in a glass jar, shake well, and use as you would regular cinnamon sugar. This is great on toast, waffles, pancakes, cereal, etc.

BANANA BREAD MUFFINS

1 ¾ c.	Whole-wheat flour
	(pastry setting, if possible)
1 tsp.	Aluminum free baking powder
½ tsp.	Baking soda
¼ tsp.	Pink Himalayan or unrefined sea salt
3	Bananas - mashed
⅓ c.	Raw unfiltered honey
	(or real maple syrup)
¼ c.	Melted butter
2	Eggs
½ c.	Crushed pecans or chocolate/carob chips
	(optional)

INSTRUCTIONS

1. Combine all ingredients except flour and mix well.
2. Add flour slowly and mix until lumps are gone.
3. Fill muffin cups, with or without liners (I used the little teeny mini-muffin cups).
4. Bake at 350° F for 15-20 minutes or until the top bounces back when touched.

Don't over-bake these. They're so much better when they're super moist!

*Note: If you have dehydrated bananas, you can reconstitute them (equivalent to two bananas) by soaking them in warm water until soft and then mashing them. You can also use dehydrated butter and eggs, if you're in an emergency situation and can't get fresh.

BANANA BREAD

3	Very ripe bananas
½ c.	Real butter
2	Eggs, beaten
1 c.	Coconut palm sugar
1 tsp.	Baking soda
½ tsp.	Unrefined salt
½ c.	Chopped pecans - optional
	(or healthy mini chocolate chips)
1¾ c.	Whole-wheat flour

INSTRUCTIONS

1. Combine ingredients and pour into two 9 x 5 bread pans.
2. Bake at 350° F for 25 minutes. Then lower the temperature to 275° F and bake for another 20 minutes.

BLUEBERRY MUFFINS

4	Eggs
2 c.	Un-refined sugar
1 c.	White bean puree
1 tsp.	Vanilla
3 ¾ c.	Whole-wheat flour
1 tsp.	Sea or Pink Himalayan salt
1 tsp.	Baking soda
2 c.	Sour cream
2 c.	Blueberries

INSTRUCTIONS

1. Preheat oven to 400° F.
2. Grease 24 muffin cups lined with paper liners.
3. In large bowl, beat eggs, sweetener, sour cream, water (if using powdered foods), vanilla, and bean puree.
4. In separate bowl, stir together flour, salt, and baking soda.
5. Stir dry ingredients into egg mixture. Slowly, and mix well. Gently fold in drained blueberries.
6. Scoop batter into prepared muffin cups (about ¾ full)
7. Bake for approximately 20 minutes or until middle bounces back when poked.

FLUFFY CLOUD BREAD / BUNS
(Fun for kids and the whole family!)

3	Eggs, separated (very carefully)
3 Tbsp.	Cottage cheese or cream cheese (homemade or good organic with no other junk ingredients)
¼ tsp.	Cream of tartar
1 tsp.	Raw honey or powdered coconut palm sugar

INSTRUCTIONS

1. In one bowl, mix egg yolks, cottage/cream cheese, and sweetener.
2. In blender, mix egg whites and cream of tartar. Beat on high until it's fluffy and nice peaks form.
3. Very carefully fold yolk mixture into egg white mixture until mixed, but don't break down the fluffiness.
4. Lightly grease baking pans with coconut oil or butter.
5. Scoop mixture with large spoon onto pan and spread out to size of round hamburger bun (approximately ¾" thick and 5" wide).
6. Bake on middle rack at 300° F for approximately 30 minutes (could be less, could be more). Watch for them to become a light golden brown.
7. Remove from pans and transfer to cooling rack.

At first, the consistency is similar to a flaky meringue. Once completely cooled and put into bag or airtight container overnight, they'll transform more into the consistency of bread.

CINNAMON CARAMEL ROLLS

4 c.	Very warm water
2 Tbsp.	SAF brand yeast
	(If you're using commercial yeast, I'm currently transitioning to homemade "Pioneer" yeast.)
½ c.	Extra virgin olive oil or melted coconut oil
	(I use organic from Costco)
½ c.	Raw honey or maple syrup
2 Tbsp.	Pink Himalayan pink salt
1-2 Tbsp.	Raw unfiltered vinegar
	(such as Braggs)
8-12 c.	Fresh ground whole-wheat flour

Sometimes I add a little oatmeal, flax seed, chia seeds, etc., depends on my mood for the day!

INSTRUCTIONS

1. Mix everything except salt and flour for about 10 seconds in a mixer (Bosch is best).
2. Add half the flour (4-5 cups) and then the salt.
3. Mix for a minute to incorporate salt, then add the rest of the flour, cup by cup.
4. As soon as the dough starts to pull away from the sides and wipe the bowl clean down near the bottom, stop adding flour. (If it starts to stick again, add a little more until it comes clean, ¼ cup at a time.)
5. Knead in mixer or by hand (I use my Bosch) for about 10-12 minutes.
6. Roll out on counter (covered with coconut or olive oil) into a rounded rectangle, fairly thin (about ⅓" to ½" thick). It should be HUGE! Like nearly two feet wide. This makes close to 3 dozen rolls.

CINNAMON ROLL FILLING

1+ stick	REAL butter
2 c.	Coconut palm sugar
1 ½ Tbsp.	Cinnamon
	(Ceylon cinnamon is best but not necessary)
	Crushed pecans
	(optional)
	Raisins
	(optional)

INSTRUCTIONS

1. Spread butter over top, then sprinkle with sugar/cinnamon mixture. Add raisins / nuts if using them. Start rolling up into a tight roll like a long snake. Pinch edges to keep closed.

2. Using the floss method – slide floss under roll and criss-cross over top of roll, pulling tight; slice ¾" to 1" slices and lay them about 2" apart on baking sheet.

3. Turn on the oven to 125° to 170° F and let warm up for 2-3 minutes. Once you feel it getting a little warm, put cinnamon rolls in oven, turn oven OFF, and let rise till double in size.

4. Once cinnamon rolls are double (they should be touching or close to touching), turn oven on to 350° F and LEAVE rolls IN the oven, even while it's heating up. Turn on timer for 30 minutes and let bake.

TOPPING RECIPE
(Add before or after they're done baking. I prefer after.)

1 c.	Butter
1 c.	Coconut palm sugar

INSTRUCTIONS

1. Bring to boil, stirring constantly until thick.
2. Let cool for 5-10 minutes, then drizzle over top of cinnamon rolls.
3. Sprinkle crushed pecans over the top, and you're done!

FRENCH TOAST #1
("A little of this and a little of that")

6-8 slices	Homemade whole-wheat bread slices
3 Tbsp.	Raw coconut oil
4-6	Eggs
2+ Tbsp.	Milk, any kind
2+ Tbsp.	Orange juice
1+ tsp.	Vanilla
½ tsp.	Cinnamon
	(Ceylon cinnamon, if possible)
1+ Tbsp.	Real maple syrup
¼ tsp.	Unrefined salt

INSTRUCTIONS

1. Whisk above ingredients, other than bread and coconut oil, in a bowl.
2. Dip slices of bread into egg mixture and cover on both sides.
3. Heat coconut oil in pan over medium heat.
4. Lower to medium-low heat and "fry" bread slices until browned on both sides.
5. Serve with real maple syrup, raw honey, and/or fruit on top.

Can slice into dipping 'sticks' if desired.

Serve with fruit, berries, & a sprinkle of powdered coconut sugar or xylitol!

FRENCH TOAST #2

	Thick-sliced homemade whole-wheat (or other whole grain) bread
6	Eggs
2 Tbsp.	Unrefined coconut oil
¼ c.	Fresh orange juice
⅛ c.	Milk (any kind)
½ tsp.	Cinnamon (Ceylon, not cassia, if possible)
¼ tsp.	Unrefined salt

INSTRUCTIONS

1. Whisk eggs, juice, milk, cinnamon, and salt in a bowl that's wider than bread slices.
2. Dip bread into mixture and let sit for a few seconds. Make sure both sides are well coated. (It's fun to cut bread into strips for dipping, as in the photo. Kids love this!)
3. Heat coconut oil in frying pan on medium heat.
4. Add dipped bread to pan and cook well on both sides until lightly browned.

Top with your choice of toppings. Here are some favorites:
- 100% real Grade B maple syrup
- Raw honey
- Fresh fruit/berries
- Fruit sauce
- Finely chopped pecans or sliced almonds
- Unsweetened shredded coconut
- Enjoy Life brand mini chocolate chips (or homemade)
- Coconut palm sugar

PLANT BASED FRENCH TOAST

1	ripe banana
	(½ c. mashed)
1 ¼ c.	Oat or almond milk
½ Tbsp.	Flax or chia seed
¼ tsp.	Cinnamon
	(Ceylon cinnamon is better than Cassia)
½ tsp.	Vanilla extract
	(optional)
4-5 slices	Whole grain bread
	Coconut oil

INSTRUCTIONS

*Note: Thicker sturdy rustic breads work best with this recipe, but if that's not available, simply dip your bread and quickly remove it from the "egg" mixture, without letting it soak.

1. Mash banana in large shallow bowl. Add milk, flax/chia seed, cinnamon, and vanilla. Let it sit for 5 minutes. If mixture seems too thick, add more milk and stir well.
2. Heat a large sauté pan or griddle to medium/hot. Add a little coconut oil to surface for "frying".
3. Dip bread into batter and transfer to pan. Let each side cook for 3-4 minutes. Turn down heat slightly, if needed.
4. It takes longer to cook using banana/flax mixture than a real egg mixture. You may need to go a little longer, which is fine. Don't flip the bread while it's still gewey. Wait until it has browned a good bit.
5. Top with desired toppings - Real organic maple syrup, fresh fruit, peanut butter, healthy chocolate chips, etc.

TORTILLAS
(Sweet or Savory)

4 ½-5+ c.	Whole-wheat flour
	(see note at end of recipe)
1 c.	Olive or coconut oil
2 tsp.	Unrefined salt
½ c.	Raw honey
1 ½ c.	Water

INSTRUCTIONS

1. Mix flour, oil, raw honey, and salt in a mixer (3-5 minutes). Scrape sides as needed.
2. Gradually add warm water and continue mixing until dough is smooth (about 3 more minutes).
3. Add a little oil to your hands so the dough doesn't stick.
4. Divide dough into 12 equal pieces (roll into a log and cut in half; then divide those two sections in half; then divide those four sections into thirds until you have 12 pieces)
5. Roll each piece in a ball and flatten just a little bit. Let sit (covered) on a cookie sheet or plate for at least 15 minutes, up to an hour.
6. Heat tortilla maker or skillet/griddle on medium-high heat.
7. Roll out each piece with rolling pin, using coconut oil on counter to keep tortillas soft (or use tortilla maker to flatten, as I did) and cook until slightly puffy and brown (about 30-45 seconds on each side).
8. After each one is done, put on a plate and use a large pot lid to cover so they stay moist and warm.
9. Top with your favorite toppings and enjoy!

These tortillas have a slightly sweet flavor and can be used as meal tortillas or dessert tortillas. They're extremely good cut into wedges and lightly fried or baked into tortilla chips.

*Note: You may need to add more flour (and flour your surface/hands instead of oiling them) if you're using a rolling pin instead of a tortilla press.

HOMEMADE INSTANT OATMEAL PACKETS

Easy to make, fun to make, and cheap! Did you know that quick oats are simply regular oats, chopped? To make your own "instant" oats, just put them in a blender for a few seconds, and voila! Homemade instant oatmeal packets are much more filling, and you know what's in them.

Get your kids to help! Assembly line style makes this extremely fast. Just line up your little baggies and ingredients and scoop one ingredient at a time 'til you're done in all the baggies. Then move on to the next ingredient. It takes just minutes to make 30-40 packets! The baggie amounts can be doubled, if you need bigger helpings.

AFTER you've gotten all your basic flavor bags made, go back through and add your favorite flavors to them. Variations are listed below the basic recipe.

ORGANIZING YOUR PACKETS (without having to label every single bag), put all the bags of each different flavor in a plastic shoe box (or other container) and label just the box. This way, you'll know which is which, just by looking at the container.

INSTANT OATMEAL PACKET BASIC RECIPE & VARIATIONS
(Per one packet)

Mix the following in individual sandwich baggies or small mason jars:

¼ c.	Powdered oats
	(reg. oats lightly powdered in blender)
1-2 Tbsp.	Sweetener
	(I use coconut palm sugar or stevia)
1 Tbsp.	Whole powdered milk - optional
Pinch	Pink Himalayan salt

If you use a crystalized or powdered (dry) sweetener, you can add it directly to the little packets. If you use a wet sweetener (like maple, agave, etc.), then you'll want to add it after you've mixed it with hot water or milk and you're about to eat it.

TO MAKE

Add a little hot water (or milk of choice) and let it sit for a minute or two. I love to add a bit of real cream or real butter for extra flavor & creaminess.

VARIATIONS
(Adjust to your own taste / your kids' own tastes)

- **Apple-Cinnamon**: To each packet, add 1 Tbsp. sweetener, ¼ tsp. cinnamon, and 2 Tbsp. chopped dried apples
- **Apple Pie**: To each packet, add ¼ tsp. apple pie spice and a little extra sweetener
- **Brown Sugar/Cinnamon**: To each packet, add 1 Tbsp. sweetener and ¼ tsp. cinnamon
- **Raisins and Brown Sugar**: To each packet, add 1 Tbsp. sweetener and 1 Tbsp. raisins
- **Health Nut**: To each packet, add ½ Tbsp. ground flax seed, ½ Tbsp. chopped nuts/seeds of choice, and ½ tsp. chia seeds
- **Honey Nut**: To each packet, add 1 Tbsp. dehydrated honey and 1 Tbsp. chopped pecans/almonds (look for brands without all the junk or make your own; you just want plain honey powder only)
- **Fruit and Cream**: To each packet, add 2 Tbsp. dried fruit. When mixing up, add a little bit of real cream (dairy cream or coconut cream will work).
- **Maple and Brown Sugar**: To each packet add powdered/dehydrated maple syrup and extra sweetener
- **Maple Pecan**: To each packet add powdered/dehydrated maple flavoring and chopped pecans; OR add pecans to bags and just add real 100% grade B maple syrup after it's mixed with hot water.
- **Pumpkin Pie**: To each packet add ¼ tsp. pumpkin pie spice and a little extra sweetener
- **Chocolate Chip**: To each packet add healthy or homemade chocolate/carob chips

ZUCCHINI BREAD

2 ¾ c.	Fresh ground whole-wheat pastry flour
	(fresh ground is amazing)
1 tsp.	Pink Himalayan salt
1 tsp.	Baking soda
1 tsp.	Baking powder
	(aluminum free)
1 ½ tsp.	Cinnamon
	(I use Ceylon cinnamon, not Cassia, but either works)
3	Eggs
1 c.	Coconut oil
	(melted)
2 ¼ c.	Coconut sugar
3 tsp.	Vanilla extract
2 c.	Grated zucchini
1 c.	Chopped pecans

INSTRUCTIONS

1. Grease and flour two bread pans. Preheat oven to 325° F.
2. Sift dry stuff and mix wet stuff, then combine.
3. Add zucchini and nuts until well combined.
4. Pour batter in pans and bake 50-60 minute (or until toothpick comes out clean)
5. Cool in pans for 20 min, then remove bread from pans and completely cool on a rack.

SO GOOD GRANOLA!

5 c.	Regular rolled oats
½ c.	Coconut, shredded (UN-sweetened)
1 ½ c.	Sunflower seeds (or other chopped nut - raw is best)
2 Tbsp.	Ground flax / chia seeds
¾ c.	Coconut palm sugar
¾ c.	Water
¾ c.	Coconut oil or olive oil
¼ c.	Raw honey
¾ tsp.	Pink Himalayan salt or Real Salt
1 tsp.	Cinnamon
1 ½ tsp.	Vanilla

INSTRUCTIONS

1. Mix the first four ingredients in a large bowl.
2. Melt the remaining ingredients in a pot, stirring constantly until dissolved. Don't let it boil!
3. Pour over dry mix, spread in jelly roll pan (or large casserole dish) and bake at 300° F for at about 30 minutes, stirring slightly halfway through cooking. For a crunchier granola, cook longer.
4. Let cool, then add 1 ½ cups of dried fruit (cranberries, strawberries, raisins, blueberries, raspberries, unsweetened coconut, etc.) OR leave plain.
5. Store in airtight container.

This granola is SUPER yummy, cold OR hot.

SOAKED OVERNIGHT OATMEAL

½ c.	Regular oats
¾ c.	Milk (almond, cow, soy, etc.) or yogurt
1 Tbsp.	Chia seeds
2 Tbsp.	Real maple syrup or raw honey
1	Banana
	(chopped into pieces)

INSTRUCTIONS

1. Mix all ingredients in a bowl or Mason jar.
2. Cover, and let soak overnight in fridge.
3. Add a little more milk if it's too thick the next morning.

Eat as is, or add toppings.

SUGGESTED TOPPINGS
- Chopped pecans, almonds, or walnuts
- Unsweetened coconut
- Chopped fruit
- Berries
- Granola
- Raisins
- Chocolate/carob chips (kids would like this)

PANCAKES AND WAFFLES

2 c.	Whole-wheat flour
½ tsp.	Unrefined salt
1 tsp.	Baking soda
2 Tbsp.	Baking powder (aluminum free, non-GMO)
1 c.	Kefir or buttermilk
⅓ c.	Coconut oil or olive oil
4 Tbsp.	Raw honey, real maple syrup, or coconut palm sugar
1½ c.	Milk
2	Eggs
1 Tbsp.	Chia seeds

INSTRUCTIONS

1. Mix until blended
2. Grease a fry pan with coconut oil or butter and heat on medium heat. (Can also use waffle iron.)
3. Pour ¼ - ⅓ cup of batter into fry pan and cook until bubbles form, then flip to other side and cook until done.
4. Top with fruit, raw honey, maple syrup, homemade whipped cream, homemade fruit syrup, chopped nuts, unsweetened shredded coconut, homemade/healthy dark chocolate chips, cinnamon, etc.

STRAWBERRY STREUSEL MUFFINS

MUFFINS

2 ¾ c.	Whole-wheat flour
1 c.	Coconut palm sugar
2 tsp.	Baking powder (aluminum free)
½ tsp.	Baking soda
½ tsp.	Cinnamon
¼ tsp.	Unrefined salt
1 c.	Buttermilk or kefir
1	Egg
½ tsp.	Stevia powder
¼ c.	Olive oil
¼ c.	Coconut oil
2 tsp.	Vanilla
2 c.	Fresh strawberries, hulled and diced

STREUSEL

½ c.	Whole-wheat flour
¼ c.	Coconut palm sugar
½ tsp.	Cinnamon
pinch	Un-refined salt

INSTRUCTIONS

1. Preheat oven to 400° F.
2. Mix topping ingredients in separate bowl and set aside.
3. For muffins, stir dry ingredients and wet ingredients in separate bowls.
4. Combine both and stir until just incorporated. Don't overmix. Batter will be thick and lumpy.
5. Fold in strawberries.

6. Pour into muffin cups or greased muffin tin.
7. Sprinkle about 1 ½ Tbsp. of topping over top of each muffin.
8. Bake for about 20 minutes or until golden brown and toothpick comes out clean.

Let cool and enjoy!

WHOLE-WHEAT CREPES

3	Eggs
1 c.	Whole-wheat flour
	(pastry is better)
1 c.	Milk
	(any kind)
¾ c.	Water
1 Tbsp.	Raw honey
¼ tsp.	Stevia powder
1 tsp.	Vanilla
¼ tsp.	Unrefined salt
1 Tbsp.	Butter or coconut oil, melted
	(extra for cooking)

INSTRUCTIONS

1. Blend all ingredients well and let stand about 15 minutes.
2. Melt butter or oil in fry pan, over medium heat, and cover bottom of pan.
3. Pour enough batter and quicly swirl around to thinly cover bottom of pan.
4. Let cook for 1 minute and carefully flip it over to cook other side. Cook for another 30-60 seconds and remove.
5. Serve flat or rolled up with fresh fruit and maple syrup or honey.

For savory crepes, omit sweetener and add a little bit more salt. You can even add herbs. Play with it! You might be surprised by what you come up with.

Condiments, Sauces, and Mixes

KETCHUP #1

6 oz.	Tomato paste
½ c.	Water
2 Tbsp.	Raw honey, real maple syrup, or coconut palm sugar
½ - 1 tsp.	Unrefined salt
¼ + tsp.	Cumin
	(I like a little more of this stuff. YUM!)
¼ + tsp.	Dry mustard powder
¼ tsp.	Cinnamon
Pinch	Cloves
4 Tbsp.	Raw unfiltered apple cider vinegar
	(I use Bragg's)

INSTRUCTIONS

1. Mix well using a handheld blender. This will give it a smoother consistency. Play with the amounts and adjust them to your preferences.
2. If you prefer a squeeze bottle to using a spoon, you can refill a store-bought ketchup bottle by using a funnel to pour your homemade ketchup into the bottle.

To make a **dry mix** for future use, just quadruple (or more) the dry ingredients and mix well. Store in glass container. When ready to use, combine approx. 7 ½ tsp. of mix (or 2 Tbsp.+1 ½ tsp.) with tomato paste, water, and vinegar and continue with directions above.

KETCHUP #2

3 c.	Tomato paste
2 c.	Raw honey or real maple syrup
2 tsp.	Blackstrap molasses
1 c.	Water
1 tsp.	Onion powder
¼ tsp.	Garlic powder
1-1 ½ c.	Raw apple cider vinegar
4 tsp.	Unrefined salt

INSTRUCTIONS

1. Combine all ingredients in medium saucepan.
2. Simmer for 20 minutes. Let cool.
3. Store in fridge and use within about two weeks.

You can also freeze in glass canning jars, leaving ½" head space for expansion. Thaw in fridge a day or two before use.

MAYONNAISE

1 c.	Extra virgin olive oil
	(or coconut oil, if preferred)
1	Fresh egg
¼ tsp.	Mustard
	(powdered or regular)
¼ tsp.	Salt
1 Tbsp.	Raw apple cider vinegar
1 Tbsp.	Fresh lemon juice
⅛ tsp.	Paprika
1-2 tsp.	Raw honey or ⅛ tsp. Stevia

*Note: This is a slight variation to the basic but popular homemade mayonnaise recipe that is floating around the internet. I was not a fan of the internet recipe at all, so I reduced the mustard and salt measurements and added a little sweetener. Everyone has different taste preferences, so adjust as you wish!

INSTRUCTIONS

1. Add all ingredients except oil to blender. Then add ¼ c. of the oil. Turn blender on and mix well.
2. Slowly start pouring a thin stream of the remaining oil as it continues to blend. Mayonnaise will thicken up fairly quickly.
3. As soon as it's the consistency you desire, turn off the blender, spoon into a glass canning jar, and refrigerate.

RED ENCHILADA SAUCE

2 c.	Water or broth
2 Tbsp.	Olive oil
2 Tbsp.	Whole grain flour
3 Tbsp.	Chili powder
	(more or less to taste)
½ tsp.	Garlic powder
½ tsp.	Unrefined salt
¼ tsp.	Cumin
¼ tsp.	Oregano
2 Tbsp.	Raw honey
	(more or less to taste)

INSTRUCTIONS

1. Heat oil on medium-high heat in saucepan.
2. Add flour and stir over heat for 1 minute.
3. Add all remaining ingredients except water/broth and stir well.
4. Gradually add in water/broth, breaking up any clumps with a whisk.
5. Reduce heat and simmer for 10-15 minutes. If sauce gets too thick, add more liquid.

Store in refrigerator in glass jar.

BROWN GRAVY

½ c.	Whole grain flour (or bean flour)
3 c.	Water
¼ c.	Homemade mayonnaise or real food store-bought mayonnaise
1 tsp.	Unrefined salt
2 tsp.	Costco's Kirkland brand organic No Salt Seasoning Mix (or other brand seasoning)
1 ½ Tbsp.	Worcestershire sauce (I use Wizard's Organic Vegan brand)

INSTRUCTIONS

1. Blend with stick blender and simmer over medium-high heat until thick.
2. Pour over rice, potatoes, roast, etc.

Store in refrigerator in glass jar.

BASIC LIGHT GRAVY

1 quart	Vegetable or chicken broth
1 tsp.	Unrefined salt
¼ tsp.	Fresh ground pepper
2 tsp.	Costco's Kirkland brand organic No Salt Seasoning Mix
	(or other brand seasoning)
1 Tb.	Chia seeds
2-3 Tb.	Arrowroot flour or organic non-GMO cornstarch

INSTRUCTIONS

1. Dissolve arrowroot / cornstarch in a small amount of cold water. Pour into pot & combine with all other ingredients.
2. Bring to boil, stirring often, then reduce heat & let simmer until thickened.

Perfect over potatoes, brown rice, vegetables, noodles, meat, etc.
Store in refrigerator in glass jar.

CREAM OF MUSHROOM, CELERY, BROCCOLI, CHICKEN, ONION SOUP
(VERSION #1)

3 c.	Water
½ c.	Flour
	(wheat, bean, etc.)
½ tsp.	Unrefined salt
2 Tbsp.	Homemade or healthy store-bought mayonnaise
½ tsp.	Worcestershire sauce
	(optional, for extra kick)
½ c.	Mushrooms, cooked chicken, celery, broccoli, or onion – finely chopped

INSTRUCTIONS

1. Whisk water, flour, salt, mayo, and Worcestershire sauce with an electric hand blender/whisk.
2. Add mushrooms – or whichever other option you choose – and simmer until hot (and veggies are soft).

CREAM OF MUSHROOM, CELERY, BROCCOLI, CHICKEN, ONION SOUP
(VERSION #2)

*This recipe quadrupled makes 4 quarts.

3 c.	Water
½ c.	Wheat flour
	(or white bean flour, or
	3 Tbsp. arrowroot flour)
½+ tsp.	Unrefined salt
	(I also add 1 tsp. Costco's Organic
	Herb mix)
2 Tbsp.	Homemade or healthy store-bought
	mayonnaise
½ c.	Finely chopped mushrooms, celery,
	broccoli, onions, etc.
1 Tbsp.	Butter or coconut oil

INSTRUCTIONS

1. Sautee vegetables in butter/oil in large saucepan until softened.
2. Add rest of ingredients and mix well.
3. Simmer until thick, stirring occasionally.

Let cool for a few minutes, then pour into glass jars. Use just like any cream soup. Can also be put in freezer once it's cooled completely. Unthaw in fridge for 1-2 days prior to use. (Leave 1" head space for expansion)

½ tsp. guar gum or 1 tsp. chia seeds can be added to thicken even more.

SOUTHERN SECRET FRY SAUCE

| ½ c. | Homemade or healthy store-bought mayonnaise |
| ½ c. | Homemade ketchup (or organic store brand) |

INSTRUCTIONS

Mix well and use as a dip for potato fries, sweet potato fries, chicken nuggets, cut veggies, etc.

AMAZING SPINACH DIP

¼ - ½ c.	Fresh Parmesan cheese
1 c.	Sour cream
1 c.	Homemade mayonnaise
	(or real food store-bought mayonnaise)
2 tsp.	Minced garlic
2 tsp.	Worcestershire Sauce
1	Green onion, minced
10-12 oz.	Frozen chopped spinach
	(or fresh cooked and cooled)
⅔ Tbsp.	Costco's Kirkland brand organic No Salt Seasoning
	(or other favorite seasoning)
½-1 tsp.	Pink Himalayan salt
1 can	Finely chopped chestnuts (optional)

BONUS INGREDIENT

1 tsp.	Plant Therapy's Spinach Dip Mix
	(optional but yummy!)

INSTRUCTIONS

1. Thaw and squeeze all water out of spinach.
2. Mix spinach, sour cream, and mayonnaise.
3. Add rest of ingredients and mix well.

Chill well. Flavors will be enhanced as it sits for a while.

RANCH DRESSING / MIX

4 Tbsp.	Chives
4 Tbsp.	Parsley
4 Tbsp.	Dill weed
2 Tbsp.	Garlic powder
2 Tbsp.	Onion powder
1 Tbsp.	Unrefined salt
1 Tbsp.	Pepper

INSTRUCTIONS

Mix the following dried herbs, etc. Store herb mixture in glass jar.

To use, mix 2 ¼ tsp. dry mix to the following:
- **Dip** – 1 c. healthy mayonnaise and ½ c. sour cream
- **Dressing** – 1 c. healthy mayonnaise and ½ c. buttermilk or kefir

CATALINA DRESSING

½ c	Homemade or healthy store-bought ketchup
½ c.	Raw honey or real maple syrup
½ c.	Apple cider vinegar or red wine vinegar
½ tsp.	Onion powder
½ tsp.	Paprika
½ tsp.	Worcestershire sauce (I use Organic Wizard brand)
1 c.	Extra virgin olive oil
	Salt and pepper to taste

INSTRUCTIONS

1. Add the ketchup, sweetener, vinegar, onion powder, paprika and Worcestershire to a food processor bowl.
2. Pulse until blended.
3. With the processor running, slowly add the oil. Check the seasonings and add more if needed. (This is very much a "personal taste preference" recipe.)

Cover and refrigerate until ready to use.

BALSAMIC DRESSING

1 Tbsp.	Plain mustard
½ tsp.	Unrefined salt
½ c.	Extra virgin olive oil
½ tsp. (1 clove)	Garlic, mashed to paste
3 Tbsp.	Balsamic vinegar
1 tsp.	Lemon juice
3 Tbsp.	Fresh, chopped basil
2 Tbsp.	Parmesan cheese
¼ tsp.	Black pepper

*Can substitute with raw apple cider vinegar if desired. Can also add raw honey if you want a slightly sweet undertone. Play with it!

INSTRUCTIONS

Mix with a hand immersion blender until well combined. Refrigerate in glass jar.

RASPBERRY PECAN VINAIGRETTE

¼ c.	Extra virgin olive oil
¼ c.	Braggs raw apple cider vinegar
¼ c.	Raspberries
	(or other berry)
¼ c.	Raw honey
1-2 tsp.	Lemon juice
¼ tsp.	Pink Himalayan or sea salt

INSTRUCTIONS

Mix with a hand immersion blender until well combined. Refrigerate in glass jar.

HONEY MUSTARD BALSAMIC DRESSING

¼ c.	Raw honey
⅛ - ¼ c.	Dijon or other good mustard
½ - ¾ c.	Balsamic vinegar
½ tsp.	Chia seeds
Dash	Pepper

INSTRUCTIONS

1. Whisk together honey and mustard until well blended, adjust amounts to taste.
2. Drizzle in the balsamic vinegar and whisk until thin enough to pour.
3. Add chia seeds and pepper and blend well.

Store in refrigerator in glass jar.

ITALIAN DRESSING AND MIX

½ Tbsp.	Garlic powder
½ Tbsp.	Onion powder
2 ½ Tbsp.	Unrefined salt
1 Tbsp.	Coconut palm sugar
2 Tbsp.	Dried oregano
¼ tsp.	Dried thyme
1 tsp.	Dried basil
1 Tbsp.	Dried parsley
⅛ tsp.	Celery seed (powdered)
1 tsp.	Black pepper

INSTRUCTIONS

Mix all ingredients in small glass jar and store. Makes ½ c. dry mix or 16 servings.

DRESSING

2 Tbsp. dry seasoning mix (above)

¼ c. raw apple cider vinegar

¼ - ½ c. extra virgin olive oil (depending on how tangy or mild you like it)

1-2 Tbsp. raw honey

2 Tbsp. Parmesan cheese (optional)

To prepare dressing, whisk together ingredients above. To make creamy Italian dressing, add 2 Tbsp. homemade or healthy mayonnaise.

Parmesan cheese acts as a slight emulsifier to keep dressing from separating as easily. ¼ tsp. of Guar gum or ½ tsp. mustard can also be used to emulsify.

POPPY SEED / CHIA SEED DRESSING

VERSION #1

1 c.	Homemade or healthy mayonnaise
2 Tbsp.	Raw honey
½ tsp.	Yellow mustard
1 Tbsp.	Raw apple cider vinegar
1 Tbsp.	Poppy seeds
	(or chia seeds)
¼ tsp.	Unrefined salt
¼ c.	Water
1 tsp.	Lemon juice
	(or extra vinegar)

VERSION #2

1 c.	Olive oil
¼ c.	Apple cider vinegar
¼ c.	Raw honey
1 ½ Tbsp.	Poppy seeds
	(or chia seeds)
⅛ tsp.	Guar gum

INSTRUCTIONS

Whisk and refrigerate until ready to use

EASY BBQ SAUCE

1 c.	Ketchup
½ c.	Raw apple cider vinegar
2 Tbsp.	Raw honey
2 Tbsp.	Molasses
2 Tbsp.	Worcestershire sauce
½ tsp.	Unrefined salt

INSTRUCTIONS

Blend and pour over meat or refrigerate until use.

HEARTY BARBEQUE SAUCE

(This recipe can be halved to make a smaller batch.)

1 qt.	Ketchup
1 c.	Finely-minced onion
1 ½ c.	Raw apple cider vinegar
¾ c.	Extra virgin olive oil
1 tsp.	Onion powder
1 tsp.	Unrefined salt
4 c.	Coconut palm sugar
	(or a combo of coconut palm sugar, raw honey, maple syrup, and/or molasses)
½ c.	Worcestershire sauce
2 ½ Tbsp.	Flour
	(to thicken)

INSTRUCTIONS

1. Mix all ingredients together in a pot and simmer for one hour.
2. Store in glass jars in refrigerator. If not using within a couple of weeks, it can be frozen. Unthaw in refridgerator for 1-2 days prior to use. (Leave 1" head space for expansion.)

FRUIT SYRUP / SAUCE

1 ½ c.	Fresh or frozen (thawed) fruit or berries (keep juice if fruit is thawed)
½+ c.	Raw honey or real maple syrup
½ tsp.	Lemon juice
¼ tsp.	Powdered stevia
2 Tbsp.	Arrowroot flour or organic corn starch
¼ tsp.	Guar gum

INSTRUCTIONS

1. Whisk everything in a pot and heat.
2. Stir often until thickened but pourable.
3. Pour over pancakes, waffles, crepes, ice-cream, etc.

HONEY SYRUP

¼ c.	Raw honey
¼ c.	Real butter or coconut oil
½ tsp.	Arrowroot
	(or organic cornstarch)
¼ tsp.	Salt

INSTRUCTIONS

Combine in saucepan and melt. Stir well and pour over whatever you're eating. Yum! Can also add mashed berries to this syrup, if desired.

FUDGE SAUCE

¾ c.	Cream
	(raw pastured cow's milk cream or coconut cream)
¾ c.	Coconut palm sugar or ½ c. raw honey
1 Tbsp.	Dark chocolate chips
	(Enjoy Life brand or homemade)
¼ c.	Real butter
2 tsp.	Vanilla

INSTRUCTIONS

1. Mix sugar, butter, and chocolate in saucepan. Melt on low.
2. Add cream and let bubble on low heat for 10 minutes. Don't stir.
3. Remove from heat, add vanilla, and stir.

Use hot, or let cool and store in glass canning jar in fridge.

Desserts and Snacks

PERFECTLY PERFECT "BLONDE" BROWNIES

2 ¼ c. w	Whole-wheat flour (pastry flour is better)
1 ½ tsp.	Baking powder
1 ½ tsp.	Pink Himalayan salt
2 ½ c.	Coconut palm sugar
3	Large eggs
1 ¼ c.	Real butter
2 ½ tsp.	Real vanilla extract
1 c.	Healthy chocolate/carob chips (optional)

INSTRUCTIONS

1. Grease a 9 x 13 baking pan with butter or coconut oil.
2. Line bottom of pan with parchment paper. Grease and flour parchment paper.
3. Cook butter over medium heat until it browns slightly. (Don't let it burn!)
4. Mix eggs, butter, vanilla, and coconut sugar in a mixer. Add rest of ingredients and mix until well combined.
5. Pour into pan and bake on 350˚ F for 35-40 minutes (or until toothpick comes out clean).
6. Let cool, cut, and enjoy!

SOUTHERN SWEET POTATO SOUFFLE

3 c.	Sweet potatoes, cooked
1 c.	Coconut palm sugar
2	Eggs
1 tsp.	Real vanilla
½ c.	Milk (any kind)
½ c.	Real butter (softened)

TOPPING:

⅓ c.	Whole-wheat flour
1 c.	Coconut palm sugar
⅓ c.	Real butter (softened)
1 c.	Chopped pecans
	Homemade marshmallows (recipe is in this book)

INSTRUCTIONS

1. Mix all ingredients (except for topping) until fluffy and pour into lightly greased casserole dish.
2. Mix topping ingredients and pour over sweet potato mixture.
3. Top with homemade marshmallows.
4. Bake at 350° F for approximately 45 minutes, or until marshmallows are well browned.

ALMOND JOYFULS

2 c.	Unsweetened shredded coconut
⅓ c.	Mild raw honey or real maple syrup
12	Whole almonds
	(optional)
6 oz.	Dark chocolate, melted
	(I use Enjoy Life brand chocolate chips)
	Stevia
	(to taste)
1 Tbsp.	Coconut oil

INSTRUCTIONS

1. Mix shredded coconut, honey/maple syrup, and stevia until very moist.
2. Put cooling rack on top of cookie sheet, roll coconut into balls or bars, and place on top of rack.
3. Put almond on top of each ball or bar.
4. Mix chocolate and coconut oil and pour over bars (or use fork to dip bars into chocolate).
5. Let drain on rack over the top of cooking sheet. Can put in refrigerator to set faster.

CHOCOLATE CHIP CHUNKIES

2 ½ c.	Whole-wheat flour
1 ⅓ c.	Real butter
1 ¾ c.	Coconut palm sugar
2	Eggs
2 tsp.	Vanilla
1 tsp.	Baking soda
1 tsp.	Unrefined salt
2 c.	Chocolate chips
	(Enjoy Life brand, homemade, or a good organic brand)
½ c.	Oats
½ c.	Unsweetened shredded coconut
¼ c.	Chopped pecans
	(optional)

INSTRUCTIONS

1. Mix well and drop by spoonfuls onto cookie sheet.
2. Bake at 375° F for 10-12 minutes.

CINNAMON SWIRL CAKE

3 c.	Whole-wheat flour, finely ground (or other whole grain)
¼ tsp.	Pink Himalayan salt (or Real Salt)
1 c.	Coconut palm sugar (organic, unrefined)
4 tsp.	Baking powder (aluminum free)
1 ½ c.	Milk (any kind - cow, goat, almond, rice, oat, etc.)
2	Eggs (farm fresh of course)
2 tsp.	Vanilla extract
½ c.	Real butter, **melted** (organic or farm fresh, if possible)
	Stevia to taste

TOPPING

1 c.	Real butter, **softened**
1 c.	Coconut palm sugar
2 Tbsp.	Whole-wheat flour (or other whole grain)
1 Tbsp.	Cinnamon
¼ tsp.	Stevia powder

INSTRUCTIONS

1. Grease 9 x 13 with coconut oil.
2. Preheat oven to 350° F. Mix all ingredients for main cake except the butter.

3. Once well combined, slowly stir in the melted butter. Pour into pan. Set aside.

FOR TOPPING

1. Mix 2 sticks softened butter, coconut palm sugar, flour, and cinnamon together until well combined and creamy.
2. Drop evenly over batter by the "Tablespoonfuls" and use a knife to marble/swirl through the cake.
3. Bake at 350° F for 35-40 minutes, or until toothpick comes out clean. Top will be crusty, middle will be a creamy, fluffy cake.

You can also try adding ½ c. raisins, pecans, chocolate chips, etc. We actually think, as yummy as this cake is, that it needs something more. So add whatever you want to add!

REAL FOOD DARK FUDGE

1 c.	Raw cacao, cocoa powder, or carob powder
½ c.	Real butter (softened)
½ c.	Coconut oil
1 c.	Mild raw honey
1 c.	Real maple syrup
2 tsp.	Real vanilla
	Stevia to taste

INSTRUCTIONS

1. Grease 8 x 8 pan.
2. Mix all ingredients in food processor or high-powered blender.
3. Spread into pan and smooth top with spoon.
4. Put in freezer for approx one hour. Cut into squares. Serve.

OPTIONAL ADD-INS

Unsweetened shredded coconut, Peanut Butter, Mint extract or essential oil

*This fudge is very dark. If it's not sweet enough, add more stevia. My young kids liked this fudge, but they're used to less sweet foods, so you may have to experiment before letting your own kids taste it.

CRISPY RUSTIC ENERGY CRACKERS

1 ½ c.	Chia seeds
¼ c.	Flax seed
¼ c.	Sesame and/or sunflower seeds
	(can use combo of both)
1 c.	Water
1 tsp.	Liquid aminos or organic soy/tamari sauce
	(we use Bragg brand)
1 ½ tsp.	Organic Worchestershire sauce
	(we use Wizard vegan brand)
½ + tsp.	Pink Himalayan or REAL salt
1 tsp.	Herb/spice mix
	(we use Kirkland brand from Costco)
½ tsp.	Garlic powder
½ tsp.	Onion powder
1 ½ + tsp.	Nutritional yeast

INSTRUCTIONS

1. Mix and let sit for about 5 mins. Preheat oven to 325° and line a large baking sheet with parchment paper.
2. Stir mixture again, and pour onto parchment paper. Spread as thin as possible onto parchment paper keeping the middle thinner than the edges. You want these as paper-thin as you can get them.
3. Sprinkle top with extra salt, herbs, or Parmesan cheese, if desired.
4. Bake for 20-30 mins, or until top is crispy.
5. Remove from oven, slice into crackers with knife or pizza/pastry cutter, and flip crackers to the other side.
6. Bake for another 20+ mins. Watch them closely. You want them to cook just until crispy, but not until they're browned on the edges.
7. Cool completely on pan, and store in airtight container. (I store mine in glass canning jars.)

THIN-WHEAT CRACKERS

IN A MEDIUM BOWL WHISK TOGETHER:

1 ½ c.	Whole-wheat or spelt flour (pastry flour is best)
¼ tsp.	Unrefined salt
¼ tsp.	Baking soda
2 Tbsp.	Dry buttermilk powder (if using fresh buttermilk, reduce amount of water)

ADD TO DRY MIX:

½ c.	Water
3 Tbsp.	Cooking oil or melted butter

INSTRUCTIONS

1. Stir until all the flour is absorbed. Don't over mix.
2. Cover the bowl with plastic wrap and let sit for about 10 minutes.
3. Divide dough in half and plop half of it on a flat cookie sheet (without edges) OR onto a silicone baking liner.
4. Cover dough with plastic wrap, the size of your pan or liner. Roll out to edges. (Dough will be VERY thin! If you're using a liner, put your liner onto a cookie sheet after rolling out the dough.) Remove plastic wrap after it's all smoothed out.
5. Using a pizza cutter, score dough into cracker squares. I make mine about 1 - 1 ½ inches.
6. Sprinkle dough squares with a GENEROUS amount of any topping you want!
   - Sea Salt
   - Garlic Salt
   - Onion Salt
   - Cinnamon Sugar

- • Crushed Herbs
- • Poppy Seeds
- • Sesame Seeds
- • Shredded or Parmesan Cheese

My personal favorite (so far) is garlic salt and parsley.

7. Bake at 350° F for about 12-15 minutes.

*Note: If your edges are too thin, they will burn easily. Try to even all the dough out to the same thickness all the way around, as much as possible. Your crackers will get crispier as they cool down.

Try them with cheese balls or cracker dip. The cinnamon ones would be great with a fruit and cream cheese ball or fruit dip. I think these are perfect for party appetizers or just in your kid's lunchbox!

Real Food Pantry Makeover

BERRY FRUIT CRISP

3-6 c.	Fresh or frozen berries or chopped-up fruit (partially thawed)*
4 Tbsp.	Raw honey or maple syrup
2 c.	Whole grain flour
2 c.	Rolled oats
1 ½ c.	Coconut palm sugar
1 tsp.	Cinnamon (Ceylon is best)
½ tsp.	Nutmeg
1 ½ c.	Butter, melted
½ tsp.	Unrefined salt
¼ tsp.	Stevia, powdered

*Amount of fruit/berries used will depend on size of baking dish.

INSTRUCTIONS

1. Stir fruit and honey/maple syrup (optional) in mixing bowl. (You may omit this sweetener if you want to just use the fruit itself.)
2. Pour into baking dish.
3. Mix rest of ingredients together.
4. Break up, crumble, and sprinkle over top of fruit.
5. Bake at 350° F for 30-40 minutes.

NO BAKE CHEWY GRANOLA BARS

6 c.	Granola
	(organic store-bought or homemade)
1 ½ c.	Raw honey
	(or ½ c. raw honey and ¼ c. maple syrup)
1 c.	Chopped almonds, pecans, peanuts, or sunflower seeds
1 Tbsp.	Chia seeds
	(optional)
1 c.	Coconut palm sugar
1 c.	Peanut or almond butter
1 c.	Dark chocolate chips
	(Enjoy Life brand or homemade is best)
Pinch	Unrefined salt

INSTRUCTIONS

1. Bring brown sugar and honey to boil in medium saucepan.
2. Remove from heat and stir in peanut butter. Add rest of ingredients.
3. Let cool a bit, and press mixture into a lightly greased large casserole dish. (9 x 13 is TOO SMALL.)
4. Put a piece of parchment paper (or wax paper) over top of bars and smooth the top as much as you can with your hand or a wooden spoon.
5. When completely cool, cut into bars and store in container.

They can be wrapped in plastic wrap or parchment paper and tied with a cute bow or label, if you want to give them away as treats.

QUICK VERSION:

I make this version more often than the other version. Just make sure to squish and smooth underneath the parchment paper really well, so the bars are compressed and tight.

INSTRUCTIONS

1. Mix all ingredients really well in a big bowl (no boiling needed).
2. Press into pan and cut as directed in original version.

Done!

CHEWY CINNAMON RAISIN GRANOLA BARS

4 ½ c.	Rolled oats
1 tsp.	Baking soda
⅔ c.	Butter, softened
⅓ c.	Coconut palm sugar
1 c.	Whole-wheat pastry flour
1 tsp.	Vanilla
½-1 tsp.	Ceylon cinnamon
	(Cassia works, Ceylon is much better)
½ c.	Raw honey
½ c.	Raisins

INSTRUCTIONS

1. Lightly grease 9 x 9 pan.
2. Combine ingredients in a big bowl and mix well.
3. Press mixture into pan and bake at 325° F for 18-22 minutes or until slightly browned.
4. Let cool, then cut into bars.

Wrap each bar, or store in container.

CANDIED PECANS

2	Egg whites
2 Tbsp.	Water
1 c.	Coconut palm sugar
1 tsp.	Unrefined salt
1 tsp.	Ceylon cinnamon (optional)
2 Tbsp.	Raw cacao or cocoa powder (optional, but yum!)
4 c. (16 oz.)	Chopped pecans

INSTRUCTIONS

1. Preheat oven to 225° F.
2. Beat egg whites and water in large bowl.
3. Add pecans and stir.
4. Whisk coconut palm sugar, salt, cinnamon, and cacao together.
5. Pour over coated pecans and stir again.
6. Spread on baking sheet that's been lightly greased with coconut oil.
7. Bake for one hour, stirring every 15 minutes.

OATMEAL CAKE

½ c.	Rolled oats
¾ c.	Boiling water
1 c.	Coconut palm sugar
⅔ c.	Whole-wheat flour
	(pastry if possible, but not required)
½ tsp.	Unrefined salt
½ tsp.	Baking soda
1	Egg
¼ c.	Shortening
	(organic non-hydrogenated such as Nutiva or Spectrum brand)

INSTRUCTIONS

1. Mix oatmeal with water in bowl and cover.
2. Mix other ingredients, then combine with oatmeal.
3. Pour into 8 x 8 pan and bake at 350° F for 23-25 minutes.

Frosting for this cake is the "Coconut Pecan Frosting" used in my chocolate cake recipe; and it is SO yummy!

CHOCOLATE CAKE

2 c.	Blanched almond flour*
¼ c.	Raw cacao powder
	(or unsweetened cocoa powder)
½ tsp.	Pink Himalayan (or unrefined sea) salt
½ tsp.	Baking soda
1 c.	100% Grade B maple syrup
	(or raw honey, which will have a
	slightly stronger flavor)
2 large	Eggs
	(I use free range organic)
1 Tbsp.	Vanilla

*I use Honeyville Farms blanched. Bob's Red Mill brand won't work well; it still has skins and is too thick.

INSTRUCTIONS

1. Preheat oven to 350° F.
2. Lightly grease 9" cake pan with coconut oil (or olive/grape seed/almond or whatever oil.)
3. Combine dry ingredients in one bowl and whisk wet ingredients (and egg) in another bowl.
4. Combine thoroughly.
5. Pour into pan and bake for 35-40 minutes, until toothpick comes out clean.
6. Let cool in pan for one hour before taking out or serving.

COCONUT PECAN FROSTING
(Like German Chocolate Frosting – but BETTER)

6 Tbsp.	Butter, melted
⅔ c.	Coconut palm sugar
1 c.	Unsweetened, shredded coconut
1 c.	Crushed pecans
4 Tbsp.	Milk
	(any kind works)
1 tsp.	Vanilla

INSTRUCTIONS

1. Combine all ingredients, mix well, and spread on top of slightly-cooled cake.
2. Broil for 1-3 minutes until browned and bubbly/crusty on top. WATCH it carefully, so it doesn't burn!

Perfect on top of the chocolate cake & oatmeal cake!

BETTER THAN MICROWAVE POPCORN
("A little of this and a little of that")

Air popped popcorn

Coconut oil

(or real butter, but coconut oil is amazing!)

Seasoned salt

(such as Pink Himalayan salt mixed with Costco's
Kirkland brand organic 21 herb and spice mix)

INSTRUCTIONS

1. Melt oil or butter over low heat, pour over popcorn, and stir well.
2. Add seasoned salt and stir again.

Enjoy!

UN-CRACKER JACKS

Remember those, my 80's friends? The little prize in the box? Yep those! These taste the same, but better!

	Air popped organic popcorn
	(a good-sized bowl full; remember to remove the un-popped kernels)
1 c.	Real butter
1 c.	Coconut palm sugar
Pinch	Unrefined salt
½ c.	Plain roasted peanuts
	(optional)

INSTRUCTIONS

1. Bring butter, coconut sugar, and salt to a boil.
2. Keep boiling until it becomes very thick like a runny caramel (close to soft ball stage with a candy thermometer; remember to stir so it doesn't burn).
3. Pour caramel mix over popcorn. Add peanuts. Stir well.
4. Choose your option:

OPTION #1

Eat immediately while warm and chewy

OPTION #2

Let cool slightly, cover, and wait several hours. Popcorn will harden up just like the real thing.

Get yourself some Chinese take out boxes from your local craft store (or online), fill them up with Un-Cracker Jacks, and treat yourself to a movie!

SIMPLICITY AT ITS FINEST
("A little of this and a little of that")

Strawberries

Bananas

Chopped Pecans

Carob Chips

(or dark chocolate chips, Enjoy Life brand or homemade)

INSTRUCTIONS

1. Mix.
2. Eat.
3. Smile.
4. Repeat.

BERRIES AND CREAM SCONES

2 c.	Whole-wheat flour
½ c.	Coconut palm sugar
1 tsp.	Baking powder (aluminum free)
¼ tsp.	Baking soda
½ tsp.	Unrefined salt
8 Tbsp.	Butter (frozen)
½ c.	Berries (or cut up fruit such as peaches or strawberries)
½ c.	Sour cream
1	Egg
½ + tsp.	Stevia
8 oz.	Cream cheese (cut into small chunks)

INSTRUCTIONS

1. Mix all dry ingredients.
2. Grate butter into flour mixture with large-hole-side of grater. Work into mixture with hands until crumbly.
3. Whisk sour cream and egg in small bowl until smoothe.
4. Using a fork, stir egg mixture into flour mixture until large clumps form. Add fruit and cream cheese chunks and stir until lightly incorporated.
5. Scoop 2" balls of dough with a large spoon and put onto cookie sheet. Press in the middle to flatten slightly.
6. Sprinkle with more coconut palm sugar and bake at 400° F for 15-17 minutes.

JENNIFER'S EXCLUSIVE
CHEWY CHOCOLATE CRACKLE COOKIES

Real, authentic, chewy on the inside, crusty on the outside, chocolate cookies with chocolate chips! No one will even know that they're not junk food! (Unless you tell them. Which would probably be a good idea, so people know that healthy food tastes great!)

1 c.	Almond butter
1 c.	Coconut palm sugar
2	Eggs, beaten
½ c.	Raw cacao powder, carob powder, or baking cocoa
1 tsp.	Baking soda
1 tsp.	Vanilla (or ⅓ of the seeds in a vanilla bean)
⅛ c.	Real maple syrup
⅛ tsp.	Green stevia herb (powdered - or a couple squirts of stevia extract, if you don't have fresh herb)
Pinch	Unrefined salt
2-4 Tbsp.	Milk (any kind should work: almond, cow, rice, goat, etc.)
¼ c.	Enjoy Life brand mini chocolate chips (optional)

INSTRUCTIONS

1. Mix together everything but the chocolate chips and milk.
2. Slowly add the milk. (The amount of milk you use could vary. You may use more or less. Dough should be fairly soft like regular cookie dough, and a little bit shiny after it's all incorporated - but not runny.)

3. Add the chocolate chips and mix everything really well.
4. Scoop onto cookie sheet using a 1" cookie scoop.
5. Bake at 350˚ F for 10-11 minutes.

*TIP: For a soft Oreo®-like sandwich cookie, make the homemade marshmallow recipe (below) and spread it between two cookies before it has set into marshmallows. Oh my goodness . . . heaven!

NEARLY BOXED BROWNIES

Use the same recipe as the "Chewy Chocolate Crackle Cookies" (above); but this time add more milk, until the consistency is not runny but softer and spreadable in a 9 x 13 glass dish. Bake at 350° F for 15-25 minutes or until toothpick comes out clean. (Under-baked and gooey in the middle is best, just like "junk food" brownies. Top should be crusty and crackled.)
That's it!!!

MARSHMALLOWS

1 c.	Filtered water
	(split in half)
3 Tbsp.	Gelatin
	(organic grass-fed, if possible;
	but regular works, too.)
1 c.	Organic raw honey or maple syrup
1 tsp.	Vanilla
¼ tsp.	Unrefined salt

INSTRUCTIONS

1. Grease an 8 x 8 pan (or larger; I used coconut oil, but it doesn't matter). Line with parchment or wax paper in both directions

2. In a mixer bowl, combine gelatin and ½ c. water. Let sit.

3. Pour the other ½ c. water in a sauce pan with honey/agave, vanilla, and salt. Turn the burner to medium-high heat, bringing to a boil.

4. Place candy thermometer in the sauce pan and continue to boil until it reaches 240° F, about 7-10 minutes. Remember to keep stirring, so it doesn't burn!

5. Turn your mixer on to low/medium speed and beat while pouring sweet mixture into softened gelatin.

6. Turn mixer to high and continue beating until it becomes thick like marshmallow crème, about 8-10 minutes.

7. Transfer marshmallow crème to lined pan and smooth top with a spatula. This sets up FAST, so it's hard to get it completely smooth. You can lightly grease your hands or spatula with coconut oil to smooth more, if needed.

8. Let set for a few minutes, cut into squares, and enjoy!

These can be used exactly like you would use marshmallows in any recipe!

*Note: You can lightly dust these with cornstarch or arrowroot powder to reduce stickiness, or you can use xylitol, so it's sweeter. I'm not a big xylitol fan, but I do use it on rare occasion. Just powder it in a blender, and dust it over your marshmallows. Xylitol will give it a slightly cool sensation. Honestly, we didn't care that ours were a little sticky.

GENTLY "FRIED" POTATO CHIPS
("A little of this and a little of that")

This makes for a great breakfast (an alternative to hash browns), snack, or lunch/dinner.

Red or gold potatoes

Coconut oil

Unrefined salt / seasoned salt / herbs

Crushed pepper

INSTRUCTIONS

1. Thin sliced potatoes (or your favorite type of potato) with a Mandolin slicer.
2. Heat up coconut oil in a large fry-pan to medium heat (I think I started with about 2-3 Tbsp. and added more as needed).
3. Sprinkle unrefined, organic, seasoned Pink Himalayan salt (or un-seasoned) & pepper, herbs, etc., into melted coconut oil.
4. Place a layer of potato slices into the pan. Pour a little more salt on top of potatoes.
5. Keep heat at a medium-low to medium temperature (just enough to sizzle) and let potatoes brown on each side. Sprinkle with more salt & herbs if desired.
6. Once brown and slightly crispy (or as crispy as you want them), remove them from the pan and indulge!

I make sure to "fry" my foods on lower heat. More like sauté. It takes a little longer, but it's healthier. We either make our own ketchup or purchase a good, un-refined, organic brand from the natural food store; and these potatoes are DIVINE with a good ketchup!

Drinks

R.E.A.L. FRESH LEMONADE

4-7 Tbsp.	Lemon juice
	(depends on taste preference)
4 ½ c.	Water
¾ c.	Raw honey, maple syrup, or other
	liquid whole food sweetener

INSTRUCTIONS

1. Squeeze lemons and add with sweetener to water.
2. Mix well and pour into cups over ice.
3. Top with raspberries or strawberries, if desired.

HEALTHY APPLE CIDER LEMON DRINK

1 c.	Water
2 tsp.	Fresh squeezed lemon juice
1 Tbsp.	Raw apple cider vinegar
	(with the "mother," such as the
	Braggs brand)
1"-2"	Piece fresh ginger, peeled
Pinch	Cayenne pepper
	(or as much as you can handle)
	Raw honey or stevia to taste

INSTRUCTIONS

1. Mix all ingredients except sweetener in a saucepan and simmer on low for 10-15 minutes.
2. Remove ginger and pour into mug.
3. Add sweetener and sip often.

Great for nausea, sore throat, and acid reflux (heart burn).

HOT CHOCOLATE

4 c.	Milk
	(dairy or non-dairy is fine)
4 Tbsp.	Raw honey or maple syrup
2 Tbsp.	Pure vanilla
8 Tbsp.	Raw cacao / cocoa powder
¼ - ½ tsp.	Stevia
	(to taste)

INSTRUCTIONS

1. Whisk in pot on stovetop (hand immersion blender works well).
2. Heat thoroughly until tiny, fine bubbles form on edges.
3. For flavor variation, add a tiny bit of peppermint or orange extract or essential oil. Top with fresh whipped cream, if desired.

CHOCOLATE SYRUP
(For chocolate milk or pouring over desserts)

1 c.	Water
¼ - ⅓ c.	Raw cacao, cocoa powder, or carob powder
¼ tsp.	Vanilla
½+ c.	Organic Grade B maple syrup or raw honey to taste
Pinch	Unrefined salt
½ tsp.	Guar gum
Pinch	Stevia

INSTRUCTIONS

1. Mix all ingredients and heat over stove until boiling.
2. Whisk constantly until slightly thickened, adding a little more guar gum if it's not thickening like it needs to. Using a whisk prevents it from getting clumpy. For even smoother texture, blend in a high powered blender such as Blendtec or Vitamix.
3. Let it cool a little, and then pour it into a glass jar or other pourable container.
4. Store in refrigerator. It will thicken more as it sits.
5. Add 2-3 Tbsp. of syrup to a cup of milk, stir, and enjoy!

ALMOND, NUT, AND GRAIN MILK – EASY!

1 c.	Soaked and dehydrated almonds (not required to be soaked/dried, but preferred)
4 c.	Water
	A little sweetener to taste (raw honey, maple syrup, or stevia)
Pinch	Unrefined salt

FLAVOR VARIATIONS*:

Vanilla

Chocolate/Carob

Cinnamon

*Add according to taste preferences.

INSTRUCTIONS

1. Add all ingredients to a high-powered blender, such as Blendtec or Vitamix. Blend for 2-3 minutes.
2. Strain through super fine cheese cloth or nut milk bag. (Some people don't like to strain, but it's up to you. If you do strain, the pulp can be used for smoothies, cookies, crusts, etc.)
3. Refrigerate if not used immediately.

Oat milk, cashew milk, etc., can be made using the same basic concept. Play with it!

Main and Side Dishes

HEARTY WHOLE FOOD SOUP
("A little of this and a little of that")

I'm estimating measurements in this recipe just for you. I'd say there's between ½-2 cups of each item. This is TOTALLY a make-up-the-recipe-as-you-go thing. I think I've made somewhere between 10 and 1,473 versions of this soup now.

It can be made with or without meat. And you can use meat broth, vegetable broth, or water. So if you're vegetarian or not, this works either way! It can also be made gluten-free by substituting with GF grains.

Whole grains are an awesome substitute for meat. So are kidney and black beans. They take on the flavor of whatever you add, and the texture is very similar.

The great thing about this soup is you can use fresh, frozen, or dehydrated beans and veggies (or canned if that's your only option). It's a perfect food storage soup.

	Broth or water
	(I fill the pot about ⅓ - ½ of the way full)
2 c.	Tomato sauce or tomato soup
½ c.	Barley
½ c.	Brown rice
½ c.	Any whole grain or noodles
1-2 c.	Corn
1-2 c.	Black beans
1-2 c.	Kidney or red beans
1 c.	Diced tomatoes
½ c.	Chopped carrots
½ c.	Chopped celery
1 c.	Chopped potatoes
½ lb.	Ground or shredded meat of choice
	(optional)
	Sprinkles of parsley, garlic, onion, basil, bay leaf, thyme, rosemary, marjoram
	Fresh ground pepper
	Pink Himalayan salt

INSTRUCTIONS

1. Fill your pot ½ - ⅔ full with water or broth. Add however much you want of any or all of the remaining ingredients. The measurements given are ESTIMATES!
2. Make sure to add spices and herbs the last 15 minutes of cooking for fullest flavor.
3. Cook in slow cooker for a few hours or on low on the stovetop for 1½-2 hours.

BUTTERNUT SQUASH SOUP

2 lb.	Butternut squash
	(seeded and cut into cubes)
1	Apple, finely chopped
1	Sweet onion, finely chopped
2 tsp.	Unrefined salt
8	Sage leaves
2 Tbsp.	Butter
	(or coconut oil)
½ c.	Cream
	(optional)
¼ tsp.	Pepper
1	Carrot, finely chopped
4 c.	Water, stock, or broth

INSTRUCTIONS

1. Melt butter/coconut oil in large pot and cook vegetables for 5 minutes or until lightly browned.
2. Pour in enough water/stock to cover vegetables. Bring to boil.
3. Reduce heat to low, cover, and let simmer 40 minutes or until all vegetables are tender.
4. Transfer to blender (or use immersion hand blender) and blend until smooth, adding more water/stock as needed for consistency.
5. Season more with salt, pepper, and herbs, if needed. (I like to use Costco's Kirkland brand organic No Salt Seasoning.)
6. Top with toasted pumpkin seeds, if desired.

LENTIL SOUP

2 c.	Lentils
1	Chopped onion
2 tsp.	Chili powder
2 ½ tsp.	Unrefined salt
	(we use Pink Himalayan)
1 ½ tsp.	Cumin
2	Crushed garlic cloves
2-3 c.	Stewed chopped tomatoes
	(depending on your taste buds)
7-8 c.	Water or broth
2 c.	Shredded zucchini
2 c.	Corn
	(optional)

INSTRUCTIONS

1. Sauté onion in a bit of coconut oil or butter.
2. Add rest of ingredients, cover, and simmer for approximately 60 minutes, or until beans/grains are tender.
3. Top with toasted pumpkin seeds, if desired.

CHILI – TACO SOUP
("A little of this and a little of that")

⅓ - ½ pot	Water or broth
2-3 c.	Tomato sauce or soup
	Chia seeds
	Onion, finely chopped
	Quinoa, millet, or brown rice
	Green beans
	(optional)
	Chili or taco seasoning to taste
	(homemade or healthy store-bought)
	Fresh ground pepper
	Unrefined salt
	Cooked beans
	(kidney, pinto, or black)
	Chicken
	(optional; can leave out for vegetarian soup)

INSTRUCTIONS

1. Combine in whatever amounts you choose and cook on medium-low heat for about an hour.
2. Serve with tortilla chips, sour cream, cheese, etc.

POTATO SOUP
("A little of this and a little of that")

⅓ - ½ pot	Water or broth
	Lots of potatoes, cut into small chunks
	Chia seeds
	Onion, finely chopped
	Kale, chopped
	Parmesan cheese
	Cheddar cheese
	(can be added after it's done cooking)
	Pepper
	Unrefined salt
	Herb seasoning mix, such as
	Costco's Kirkland brand

INSTRUCTIONS

1. Combine your chosen amounts of each ingredient in a big pot and cook on medium-low for 1-2 hours, depending on the size of your potato chunks.
2. Serve plain or with cheddar cheese and sour cream.

SAUTÉED RAINBOW CHARD
(OR ANY GREENS!)
("A little of this and a little of that")

Sauté any type of greens over medium-low heat with olive oil, raw apple cider vinegar, and a little Pink Himalayan salt until tender.

That's it! (If you don't like vinegar, you can just leave it out.)

This is amazing over brown rice.

SWEET AND TANGY BROCCOLI SALAD

3 bunches	Broccoli, chopped
1 c.	Chopped pecans, almonds, or sunflower seeds
1 Tbsp.	Chia seeds
1 small	Sweet onion, finely chopped
1 c.	Raisins
1 c.	Grapes or apple chunks
¼ c.	Shredded cheese (optional)

SAUCE:

1 ¾ c.	Homemade or real food store-bought mayonnaise
¼ c.	Raw honey
¼ c.	Raw apple cider vinegar
½ tsp.	Unrefined salt

INSTRUCTIONS

1. Prepare all ingredients for salad and mix together in large bowl.
2. In a separate bowl, add together the ingredients for the sauce. Mix well.
3. Toss the sauce into the salad. (Sauce may settle to bottom, so stir again before serving.)

RASPBERRY SPINACH SALAD WITH RASPBERRY PECAN VINAIGRETTE
("A little of this and a little of that")

Spinach

Raspberries

Blueberries

Carrots

Sunflower seeds

Pine nuts

Kidney beans

Black beans

Mozzarella cheese

Raspberry Pecan Vinaigrette

(recipe in the "condiments" section)

INSTRUCTIONS

1. Prepare and layer or combine all ingredients, use any amount you choose.
2. Prepare dressing and drizzle over salad.

Enjoy!

MAPLE LIME BERRY QUINOA SALAD

B.R.E.A.K.F.A.S.T. S.N.A.C.K.   H.E.A.L.T.H.Y.
L.U.N.C.H.   D.E.S.S.E.R.T.   A.D.D.I.C.T.I.N.G.
D.I.N.N.E.R.   D.E.L.I.C.I.O.U.S. E.A.S.Y.

1 ½ c.	Dry quinoa, rinsed
2-4 c.	Fresh berries
	(blueberries, raspberries, strawberries, etc.)
½ c.	Chopped pecans or almonds
¼ c.	Unsweetened shredded coconut
	(optional)
1 Tbsp.	Chia seeds

SAUCE:

4 Tbsp.	Pure maple syrup or raw honey
2 tsp.	Balsamic vinegar
2 Tbsp.	Fresh lime juice
	(or lemon, if preferred)
Good pinch	Unrefined salt
	(we use Pink Himalayan)

INSTRUCTIONS

1. Combine first five ingredients. Set aside.
2. Combine Sauce ingredients. Stir well and pour over top of cooked quinoa and fruit/nut mix.
3. Chill in refrigerator, if ingredients aren't already cold. (I rinse the quinoa in cold water, in a strainer, after it's done cooking. This cools it off a lot faster, so you don't have to wait as long to eat it!!!)

CHICKEN (OR NOT) SALAD

¼ c.	Finely chopped celery
2 c.	Finely chopped apples
1 ½ c.	Sliced almonds
2 c.	Small pasta noodles, cooked, drained, and rinsed with cold water
3-4 c.	Cooked (shredded or cubed) chicken (or add more apples and almonds for vegetarian)
1½ c.	Pineapple tidbits (finely cut pineapple)
2 c.	Grapes, halved
½ c.	Raisins (optional)
2 c.	Coleslaw or poppy seed dressing (homemade or real food store-bought)

INSTRUCTIONS

1. Combine all ingredients and mix in a large bowl.
2. Chill in refrigerator.
3. Serve plain or on bread as a sandwich.

LUSCIOUS ROASTED CAULIFLOWER

3 lbs.	Cauliflower
3+ Tbsp.	Organic extra virgin olive oil
½ tsp.	Garlic powder
¾ - 1 tsp.	Black pepper
¾ -1 tsp.	Chili powder
1 ½ Tb.	Balsamic vinegar
1 tsp.	Pink Himalayan or REAL salt

INSTRUCTIONS

1. Heat oven to 450 degrees.
2. Cut cauliflower into bite-sized pieces.
3. Drizzle with olive oil. (You may need more than 3 Tb.)
4. Add garlic, pepper, salt, & chili powder to taste. (We actually liked adding more)
5. Toss everything until well distributed.
6. Pour onto baking pan covered with parchment paper, and bake 20-30 mins, stirring a couple times. They should be well browned when finished.
7. Remove from oven, pour into bowl, & toss with balsamic vinegar.

SOUTHERN CORNBREAD

2 c.	Cornmeal
⅓ c.	Whole-wheat flour
1 ½ tsp.	Unrefined salt
2 tsp.	Baking powder (aluminum free)
1 c.	Buttermilk or kefir
½ c.	Water
2	Eggs, slightly beaten

INSTRUCTIONS

1. Mix first four ingredients together in bowl.
2. Mix last three ingredients in large bowl and add cornmeal mixture to it.
3. Put batter in prepared cast iron pan and cook at 450° F for 30-45 minutes, until browned on top. (To prepare cast iron frying pan, heat in oven ahead of time. Add 2 Tbsp. coconut oil – or pasture-raised, organic bacon grease, if you're deeply and devoutly Southern – and heat before adding batter.)

SOUTHERN CORNBREAD DRESSING

6 c.	Cornbread crumbs
1 tsp.	Black pepper
3-4	Eggs, beaten
1 ½ c.	Onions, finely chopped
¾ c.	Celery, finely chopped
¼ c.	Real butter
1 ½ c.	Hot water
1 c.	Broth
	(or more water)

INSTRUCTIONS

1. Mix together first three ingredients and set aside.
2. Cook the remaining ingredients in a saucepan until onions and celery are tender.
3. Add above mixture to cornbread crumbs and mix well. If it appears too dry, add a little more hot water. If it's too soupy, add more cornbread crumbs.
4. Place in lightly greased baking dish. Bake at 375° F for 45 minutes or until brown on top.

*Tip: When we have our Thanksgiving turkey, and I make homemade turkey gravy, I add about 1 c. crumbled dressing to the gravy. It is AMAZING!

HOMEMADE REFRIED BEANS

4 c.	Cooked pinto beans
4 Tbsp.	Real butter or coconut oil
1 c.	Finely chopped onion
3-4 cloves	Garlic, finely minced
2 tsp.	Cumin
1 tsp.	Paprika
1 tsp.	Unrefined salt
1 tsp.	Chili powder
1 tsp.	Black pepper
	Milk as needed
	(water or broth can be used also, but I prefer milk)

INSTRUCTIONS

1. In large saucepan or pot, sauté onions, garlic, and butter until soft.
2. Add cooked beans, salt, pepper, spices, and enough milk/water/broth to keep them from being completely dry.
3. Bring to slow simmer and cook on low for 10-20 minutes. Stir frequently to keep from sticking. (For thinner beans, add more liquid. For thicker beans, add less liquid. This is personal preference. I like mine right in the middle.)
4. Once everything is well cooked and incorporated with your preferred consistency, use a hand blender or fork to mash beans.

ENCHILADA CASSEROLE
("A little of this and a little of that")

Corn or whole-grain flour tortilla,
    cut into bite-sized pieces
Refried Beans
Sour Cream
Enchilada Sauce
(homemade or real food store-bought)
Tomatoes, chopped
Olives, chopped
Cheese, shredded
Lettuce, shredded
Chicken, shredded
(optional)

INSTRUCTIONS

1. Layer ingredients above in a casserole dish with tortillas, beans, sour cream, and sauce on bottom; tomatoes, olives, and optional chicken in the middle; and cheese on top.
2. Cover and bake at 350° F for 30-45 minutes or until cheese is browned and bubbling.
3. Top with shredded lettuce and more sour cream / enchilada sauce, if desired.

BAKED BEANS #1

4 c.	Cooked white or pink beans
1 c.	Ketchup
	(homemade or real food store-bought)
½ c.	Raw apple cider vinegar
2 Tbsp.	Raw honey
2 Tbsp.	Molasses
2 Tbsp.	Worcestershire sauce
½ tsp.	Unrefined salt

INSTRUCTIONS

1. Put cooked beans in a pot and set aside.
2. Mix remaining ingredients together.
3. Pour mixture over cooked beans and turn on to medium heat.
4. Let simmer until sauce darkens and gets thick. (Feel free to double the sauce recipe!)

When you're needing some sanity, I give you permission to use organic canned beans. However, to make beans from scratch, refer to "preparedness" section of book. Quick instructions: Soak dry beans the night before (or at least 6 hours prior to cooking) in a pot of water and a tablespoon or so of raw apple cider vinegar. Drain, then fill pot back up with fresh water, add a tsp. olive oil, and cook until tender. (Do not add salt before they cook! This will harden them.)

BAKED BEANS #2
("A little of this and a little of that")

White beans, cooked
(enough to fill ⅓ to ½ of a large pot)
Water
Coconut palm sugar
Molasses
Ketchup
(homemade or healthy organic store-bought)
Raw apple cider vinegar
Dry mustard powder
Unrefined salt
Pepper
Worcestershire sauce
(homemade or Wizard Organic brand)
Finely chopped onion

INSTRUCTIONS

1. Place cooked beans in a large pot.
2. Pour a little water over beans and then start adding random amounts of the other ingredients (whatever "feels right" and looks good to you).
3. Cook on medium heat; when it's warm, taste test it. If it's too tart, add more sweet. If it's too sweet, add more tart.
4. Cook until thick, saucy, dark, and onions are soft.

If you really truly struggle with estimating amounts, find yourself a couple of online baked bean recipes and use those as a guideline. It's really not hard. I promise.

CREAMY POTATO CASSEROLE
("A little of this and a little of that")

Cubed potatoes
(enough to fill casserole dish)
Cream of mushroom soup
(homemade or real food store-bought)
Cream of broccoli soup
(homemade or real food store-bought)
Unrefined salt
Pepper
Onion flakes
Garlic powder
Milk

INSTRUCTIONS

1. Combine all ingredients in a large casserole dish.
2. Mix until creamy and thick.
3. Cover loosely with foil and bake at 350° F until potatoes are soft and done.

(Optional: Sprinkle layer of whole-wheat Panko crumbs over top before baking.)

SOUTHERN "FRIED" CATFISH

	Fresh catfish filets, skin off
1 c.	Buttermilk or kefir
1 ½ c.	Cornmeal
½ c.	Whole-wheat flour
1 ½ tsp.	Unrefined salt and pepper
1 tsp.	Paprika

INSTRUCTIONS

1. Pour buttermilk/kefir in a bowl and set aside.
2. Combine the dry ingredients in a medium bowl.
3. Heat ½"-1" coconut oil over medium heat in a frying pan.
4. Dip catfish filets into buttermilk/kefir, then into dry mix.
5. Cook on both sides until flakey in the middle.

HAWAIIAN CHICKEN
(Slow Cooker and Fry Pan Recipe)

2 lb.	Organic, pastured chicken breasts
1 c.	Pineapple juice
½ c.	Raw honey, real maple syrup,
	or coconut palm sugar
⅓ c.	Braggs or other organic soy sauce
	Unrefined salt and pepper

INSTRUCTIONS

IN SLOW COOKER:
1. Place chicken in slow cooker.
2. Mix juice, sweetener, and soy sauce and pour over top of chicken.
3. Sprinkle top with salt and pepper to taste and cook on high until chicken is cooked all the way through.

IN DEEP-DISH FRYING PAN:
1. Pour sauce over top of chicken.
2. Cook until chicken is browned and somewhat caramelized on both sides. (Sauce amount can be halved or chicken amount doubled, if more concentrated sauce is desired.)

BAKED OR BROILED SALMON DINNER

VERSION #1:

1 ½ c.	Raspberries
½ c.	Raw honey
1 Tbsp.	Lemon juice
	(or sliced lemons)

VERSION #2:

½ c.	Raw honey
1 tsp.	Chia seeds
1 Tbsp.	Costco's Kirkland brand organic
	No Salt Seasoning or parsley

INSTRUCTIONS

IF BAKING:
1. Place salmon filets on tin foil on a cookie sheet.
2. Brush salmon filets with butter or coconut oil and sprinkle with a generous amount of unrefined salt and pepper.
3. Mix together either version of ingredients above and pour over the top.
4. Bake at 350° F until fish is flakey all the way through.

IF BROILING:
(Watch carefully, so it doesn't burn.)
1. Broil salmon filets on top rack for about 5 minutes.
2. Carefully turn over.
3. Pour sauce of choice over top of filets.
4. Broil 5-7 minutes longer, until fish flakes easily with fork.

Serve over brown rice or baby potatoes with a side of asparagus or broccoli.

*Excellent baked on cedar wood plank or Himalayan salt block

HUSH PUPPIES
(Perfect with seafood!)

1 ½ c.	Corn meal
1 ½ c.	Water
⅓ c.	Milk
1 Tbsp.	Olive oil or coconut oil
1	Onion, finely chopped
2	Eggs, beaten
1 c.	Whole-wheat flour
3 tsp.	Baking powder
	(aluminum free)
2 tsp.	Unrefined salt
1 tsp.	Raw honey or coconut palm sugar

INSTRUCTIONS

1. Combine cornmeal and water in a pot and cook until stiff and doughy (stirring constantly) on medium-high heat.
2. Bring to boil and remove from heat.
3. Add milk, oil, and onion. Stir until smooth.
4. Add beaten eggs. Mix until well incorporated.
5. Mix flour and other dry ingredients in separate bowl, then add to wet mixture.
6. Heat 2" coconut oil (medium heat) in deep fry pan.
7. Drop by teaspoons and fry until done. (should be crusty on outside but NOT mushy on inside, similar to cornbread)

FANCY DANCY GREEN BEANS AND CARROTS

8 oz.	French style green beans (fresh or frozen)
2	Carrots, cut into thin strips
1	Onion, cut into thin stripes
8 oz.	Mushrooms, finely chopped
¼ c.	Real butter
1 ½ tsp.	Unrefined salt
½ tsp.	Herb/spice mix (like Costco's Kirkland brand organic herb mix)
¼ tsp.	Garlic powder

INSTRUCTIONS

1. Place carrots and beans in sauce pan in about 1" water; bring to a boil.
2. In a separate pan, sauté mushrooms and onion in butter for 6-8 minutes.
3. Combine both and cook for approximately 5 minutes more. Serve hot.

BROCCOLI CASSEROLE

1	Onion, finely chopped
2	Broccoli heads, finely chopped
1 ½ c.	Chicken, chopped or shredded (optional)
1 Tbsp.	Coconut or olive oil
1 batch	Cream of mushroom/chicken/broccoli/onion soup

INSTRUCTIONS

1. Sauté chicken (if using) and onion in oil until slightly browned.
2. Pour "Cream of" soup and broccoli over chicken/onion mix in skillet and simmer for about 15 minutes. (Or bake in casserole dish at 375° F for about 30 minutes.)
3. Pour over cooked brown rice, noodles, or baby potatoes and top with cheese, if desired.

VEGGIE ALFREDO

1 box	Whole-wheat/whole grain noodles (or homemade)
2 c.	Cooked vegetables (our favorite is broccoli)

SAUCE:

2 c.	Milk (any kind)
2 Tbsp.	Real butter
1 Tbsp.	Lemon juice
½ c.	Homemade mayonnaise or healthy store-bought mayonnaise
⅓ c.	Parmesan cheese
¼ c.	Whole grain flour or bean flour
1 tsp.	Unrefined salt

INSTRUCTIONS

1. Put all sauce ingredients in pan and blend with immersion hand blender.
2. Heat and let simmer for several minutes, stirring often until thick.

Serve over noodles & vegetables

CHICKEN NUGGETS

1 lb.	Organic, pastured chicken breasts
1 c.	Whole-wheat bread crumbs
	(panko crumbs are awesome!)
¼ c.	Parmesan cheese
1 tsp.	Parsley, fresh or dried
½ tsp.	Paprika
½ tsp.	Onion powder
½ tsp.	Garlic powder
½ tsp.	Unrefined salt
½ tsp.	Pepper
	Sesame seeds
	(optional)
	Whisked egg in separate bowl
	Coconut oil or real butter

INSTRUCTIONS

1. Mix all dry ingredients together in a bowl.
2. Cut chicken breasts into small, bite-sized chunks.
3. Heat oil/butter on medium in sauté/fry pan.
4. Dip chicken into egg with one hand and into dry mixture with other hand (or using fork) and coat thoroughly.
5. Add to pan and cook all the way through, until chicken is white on inside with browned coating on outside.

Serve with homemade ketchup, secret fry sauce, ranch dressing, or BBQ sauce.

SOUTHERN CHICKEN AND DUMPLINGS

3-4	Organic, pastured chicken breasts
2 c.	Whole-wheat flour
2 tsp.	Unrefined salt
1 tsp.	Herbs and spices
	(optional, but so yummy)
¼ tsp.	Pepper
	Water

INSTRUCTIONS

1. Place chicken in large pot, covered in water twice the size of the chicken. Bring to a boil.
2. Reduce to simmer for one hour.
3. Remove chicken, shred, and return good meat to water. Add salt to taste.
4. Continue to simmer on low.
5. Mix flour, herbs/spices, pepper, and 1 tsp. salt in bowl.
6. Add water and stir until biscuit thick. Not too sticky, but not too dry.
7. Flour surface, and roll out dough to ¼" thick. Cut 4-6" thick strips.
8. Add 1-3 strips at a time to pot and cook all on medium-low until liquid is creamy and dumplings are somewhat gooey.

This stuff is AMAZING reheated as leftovers and even cold. We even eat it for breakfast!

HAWAIIAN HAYSTACKS
("A little of this and a little of that")

Cream of mushroom/chicken gravy
(made from scratch or healthy store-bought)
Cold pineapple and pineapple juice
Cooked brown rice
Frozen green peas
Chopped olives
Chopped tomatoes
(grape tomatoes are the best)
Shredded cheese

INSTRUCTIONS

1. Combine equal parts cream of mushroom soup and cream of chicken soup (two versions in this recipe book).
2. Add a little pineapple and pineapple juice and stir.
3. Keep adding pineapple juice until it's a good pouring gravy consistency but not too thin. Heat thoroughly.
4. Pile up the remaining ingredients and/or any others you can think of and cover in gravy.

WHITE LIGHTENING CHILI

⅓ - ½ pot full	Broth
	(chicken or vegetable broth)
2-4	Boneless skinless chicken breasts
¼ c.	Dehydrated onion
	or ½ c. fresh onion, finely grated
4-5 c.	Cooked white beans
2 sm or 1 lg can	Green chilis
	(or use garden fresh)
1 ½ tsp.	Garlic powder
1 Tbsp.	Extra virgin olive oil
1 tsp.	Unrefined salt
1 tsp.	Cumin
¼ tsp.	Oregano
½ tsp.	Pepper
⅛ tsp.	Cayenne pepper
1 c.	Sour cream

INSTRUCTIONS

1. Add all except sour cream to pot and simmer for about an hour. (More or less beans, chicken, and onions can be added, depending on personal taste and texture preference.)
2. Add sour cream and serve.

HOMEMADE PIZZA
("A little of this and a little of that")

There's almost nothing better than homemade pizza, and there's not much of a true recipe! I use spaghetti/marinara sauce, or I mix tomato sauce with a spoonful of pizza seasoning (no junk, of course).

The crust is made with my homemade bread recipe included in this book. Roll out the dough and bake the crust for 10 minutes, then add toppings and bake at 400° F until browned on top.

My pizza may have sauce, cheese, spinach, and pasture-raised, "no junk," uncured organic pepperoni. You're welcome to leave off the meat, if you're vegetarian, and pile on the vegetables! Vegetarian is how we usually do it.

Also add olives, mushrooms, onions, carrots, zucchini, tomatoes, peppers . . . YUM! (Am I allowed to admit that I'm an anchovy fan, too? I am. I really am.)

CARROT ZUCCHINI PIZZA
(This pizza is amazing!)

1	Whole grain pizza crust (homemade if possible*)
1	Carrot, shredded
1	Zucchini, shredded
2 c.	Pizza sauce (homemade is best, of course)
2 c.	Mozzarella cheese, shredded

INSTRUCTIONS

1. Slightly bake pizza crust for about 8-10 minutes.
2. Spread pizza sauce over crust.
3. Add carrots and zucchini, then top with cheese. (For crispier veggies, add cheese first, then veggies on top.)
4. Bake at 425° F for 20 minutes or until cheese begins to brown.

*My whole-wheat bread recipe works perfect for pizza crust.

FAST AND EASY SPIRAL LASAGNA

1 box	Organic whole-wheat spiral noodles
1 quart	Organic or homemade spaghetti / marinara sauce
1 large	Shredded carrot
1 c.	Fresh baby spinach
2 c.	Organic or homemade cottage cheese
2 c.	Shredded mozzarella cheese
1 Tbsp.	Costco (Kirkland brand) Organic No-Salt Seasoning
½ tsp.	Unrefined salt

INSTRUCTIONS

1. Mix seasoning blend and cottage cheese. Set aside.
2. Layer in this order from top to bottom:
   - Spiral noodles
   - Spaghetti / marinara sauce
   - Shredded carrot
   - Spinach
   - Pink Himalayan salt
   - Cottage cheese mixture (can use more than two cups, if needed)
   - Mozzarella cheese
3. Bake at 375° F for 45-60 minutes, or until cheese is well-browned on top

*Shredded chicken can also be added, if desired. We choose to leave it out.

Natural Living

Bonus Preview To Book #2

NOURISHING SHEA/COCOA DEODORANT
(For men or women)

2 Tbsp.	Shea butter
1 Tbsp.	Cocoa butter
½-1 Tbsp.	Unrefined coconut oil
3 Tbsp.	Arrowroot powder
	(or organic cornstarch)
1 tsp.	Baking soda
1 tsp.	Redmond (bentonite) clay
15-20 drops	Colloidal silver
30-40 drops	Essential oil

INSTRUCTIONS

1. Add all ingredients (except essential oil) in a sauce pan.
2. Mix on low heat until melted and remove from heat.
3. Add essential oil and stir well.
4. Pour into a small, shallow glass, plastic jar, or empty deodorant stick. Use knife to push out air pockets.
5. Scrape evenly across top of the jar with the side of your knife and wipe around rim, if needed.
6. Refrigerate for a few minutes to thicken. Store at room temperature or cooler.
7. To use, massage a pea-size amount into under arms with fingers.

After a day or two, if deodorant feels too solid, you can do one of two things:
1. Melt and pour into empty deodorant stick for "conventional" application
2. Melt and add a little more coconut oil, colloidal silver, or essential oil to jar to thin it out a bit.

*Note: Redmond is a brand name for the generic bentonite clay.

My favorite essential oil singles and blends for deodorant:

- Plant Therapy's "Deodorizing" blend
- Plant Therapy's "Germ Fighter" blend
- Plant Therapy's "Sensual" blend
- Lavender
- Geranium
- Chamomile
- Helichrysm
- Frankincense
- Rosemary
- Clary Sage

HAND, FACE, AND BODY SCRUB
(For men and women)

¼ c.	Pink Himalayan Salt*
⅛ + c.	Sweet almond oil or other carrier oil, such as grape seed, jojoba, rosehip, or calendula
20-40 drops	Essential oil (EO)

INSTRUCTIONS

1. Mix well in small glass jar, such as a canning jar for jams.
2. Add more carrier oil, if desired. Mixture should be very wet with slight pooling of the oil.

*Super fine texture Pink Himalayan salt can be purchased through San Francisco Salt Company online.

EO singles suggestions:
- Lavender
- Frankincense
- German Chamomile
- Helichrysm
- Geranium
- Rosewood
- Jasmine

EO blend suggestions:
- Deodorizing (Plant Therapy)
- Self Esteem (Plant Therapy)
- Sensual (Plant Therapy)
- Balance (DoTERRA)
- Le Millenia (Butterfly Express)
- Release (Young Living)

BEST GLASS CLEANER IN THE WORLD

2 c.	Warm water
¼ c.	White vinegar
¼ c.	Rubbing alcohol
1 Tbsp.	Cornstarch or arrowroot powder

INSTRUCTIONS

1. Use a funnel to pour ingredients into a large spray bottle.
2. Screw on top and shake well to combine.
3. Shake before using each time, if cornstarch is settled in bottom.

Works GREAT on all glass surfaces.

Remarkable Resources

*B*onus resources for even more information on holistic living, natural healing, real food, and abundant living!

WEBSITES

- azurestandard.com (real food, bulk, and natural products)
- bountifulbaskets.org (real food co-op)
- eatwild.com (pasture-raised animal foods and grass-fed basics)
- foodbabe.com (real food)
- jenniferdayley.com (natural healing, holistic living, and real food)
- modernalternativemama.com (real food and holistic living)
- mountainroseherbs.com (herbs and spices)
- planttherapy.com (essential oils and natural products)
- realfoodsmarket.com (real food and natural products)
- realmilk.com (farm fresh milk and dairy)
- seedrenaissance.com (organic heirloom seeds, natural yeast, herbs)
- sfsalt.com (bulk Pink Himalayan salt)

DOCUMENTARIES/FILMS

- Fat Sick and Nearly Dead
- Fed Up
- Food Inc.
- Forks Over Knives
- Genetic Roulette

BOOKS

- In Defense of Food – Michael Pollan
- Living In A Higher Vibration – Beverly Kingsford (healing and holistic living) Call (208) 524-1046 to order.
- The Art of Baking Bread With Natural Yeast – Caleb Warnock and Melissa Richardson
- The Word of Wisdom - A Modern Interpretation – John A. Widtsoe

KEEP IN TOUCH

- Website: jenniferdayley.com
- Facebook: facebook.com/thehealingplace.jenniferdayley
- Twitter: The Healing Place - @jenniferdayley
- Instagram: thehealingplacejenniferdayley
- Pinterest: pinterest.com/jenniferdayley

The 10-week
REAL FOOD PANTRY MAKEOVER
Course

Includes:

1. Membership in the 'Real Food Pantry Makeover' online support group
2. Printable workbook & other great resources
3. Free printable copy of my best selling "Real Food Pantry Makeover" book
4. Access to the full 10 week audio/video course
5. Members only bonuses

Recipe Index

Recipe Index

CPSIA information can be obtained at www.ICGtesting.com
Printed in the USA
LVOW07s2338030816

498974LV00012B/213/P